THE EARLY H. G. WELLS

'The great machine that had come flying through the air
from America that morning rushed down out of the sky'

(Illustration by Edmund Sullivan to a 'Story of the Days to Come',
published in the *Pall Mall Magazine*, 1899)

The Early
H. G. Wells

A STUDY OF THE
SCIENTIFIC ROMANCES

by

BERNARD BERGONZI

MANCHESTER
UNIVERSITY PRESS

© Bernard Bergonzi, 1961
Published by the University of Manchester at
THE UNIVERSITY PRESS
316–324 Oxford Road, Manchester, 13

Printed in Great Britain by Butler & Tanner Ltd., Frome and London

FOR
MY PARENTS

Mr. Bergonzi is on the staff of the English Department at Manchester University. He has contributed to *The Review of English Studies*, *Twentieth Century*, and *The Listener*, and reviews regularly in the *Spectator* and *The Guardian*.

PREFACE

My thanks are due to Mrs Marjorie Wells and to the Executors of H. G. Wells for permission to quote from Wells's writings and to reprint the stories which form the appendix to this study; to Professor Gordon N. Ray for supplying me with photocopies of manuscript material in the University of Illinois Library, and giving me permission to quote from it; to Mr F. W. Bateson, Professor Lord David Cecil, Professor Frank Kermode, and Mr W. W. Robson, who read this book at various stages of its development and by whose suggestions I have profited; to Mr Vincent Brome for a number of helpful conversations; and to my wife, who typed the final version, read the proofs and helped prepare the index. Acknowledgements are also due to the editors of the *Critical Quarterly*, where part of Chapter II first appeared.

The quotations from Wells's fiction which appear in this book are taken from the texts of the first editions; since Wells subsequently revised certain of his novels the passages quoted may differ slightly in one or two places from those in modern editions. As Wells's novels are, for the most part, available in a variety of editions I have given chapter numbers as the source of quotations. In the case of *The Time Machine* I have followed the chapter divisions of the Heinemann edition of 1895, which is still available in a reset version.

Unless otherwise stated, the place of publication of books referred to in the notes is London.

CONTENTS

CHAPTER I

H. G. WELLS AND THE 'FIN DE SIÈCLE'

I

H. G. WELLS died in 1946 at the age of eighty. He was so much a man of the twentieth century that it is hard to believe that he started his literary career in the middle of the eighteen-nineties. The author of the *Outline of History* and *The Shape of Things to Come* appears, at first sight, to have nothing in common with the world of *The Green Carnation* and *The Yellow Book*. Wells, the tireless designer of scientific utopias, rather despised art, while the men of the nineties lived for it. The robust creator of Kipps and Mr Polly manifestly does not belong in the shadowy gallery peopled by such exotic and attenuated figures as Dorian Gray, Aubrey Beardsley, Enoch Soames and Ernest Dowson (with the passing of time the real and the fictitious names become strangely confused). Nevertheless, Wells did begin life as a writer in, if not quite of, the eighteen-nineties. If, like his friend Stephen Crane, he had died in 1900 he would already have been established as the author of more than a dozen short novels and collections of stories or essays. Had Wells's career been truncated in this fashion he would be remembered primarily as a literary artist and hardly at all as a publicist and pamphleteer. In 1900 Wells had scarcely embarked on the self-appointed task of educating humanity that was to take up most of his time and energy during the next four decades.

In the course of this study I hope to show why Wells

could be considered an artist in the first few years of his career. It must be admitted that he was temperamentally alien to the self-conscious aestheticism that is thought of as a characteristically *fin de siècle* phenomenon, and which is inevitably associated with the names of Oscar Wilde and Aubrey Beardsley, despite the personal antipathy that existed between the two men. There were, however, occasional points of contact between the young Wells and the aesthetic *milieu*. In 1897 Wilde, writing to Robert Ross from Reading Gaol, remarked, 'you mentioned Henley had a protegé':[1] this was Wells, whose first novel, *The Time Machine*, had been serialized by W. E. Henley in *The New Review*. In a letter of October 1896, Beardsley referred to *The Island of Dr Moreau* as 'certainly a horrible affair and very well set forth'.[2] Wells himself contributed a short story to *The Yellow Book*, though admittedly to one of the more respectable numbers that appeared after Beardsley had severed his connection with it. He was sufficiently aware of the excesses of contemporary aestheticism to be able to satirize them. In a sketch called 'A Misunderstood Artist', first printed in 1894 and then included in his collection of essays, *Select Conversations with an Uncle* (1895), he describes an imaginary encounter with a cook who is an extreme devotee of *l'art pour l'art*:

Then I produced some Nocturnes in imitation of Mr Whistler, with mushrooms, truffles, grilled meat, pickled walnuts, black pudding, French plums, porter—a dinner in soft velvety black, eaten in a starlight of small scattered candles. That, too, led to a resignation: Art will ever demand its martyrs.

Here we have a remarkable though presumably inadvertent echo of the famous all-black banquet given by the Duc Jean des Esseintes in that bible of the aesthetic movement, Huysmans' *A Rebours*. The cook continues, insisting on the absolute separation of art from all practical or moral considerations, in a way which is uncomfortably close to some of the exchanges at Wilde's trials:

My dinners stick in the memory. I cannot study these people—my genius is all too imperative. If I needed a flavour of almonds and had nothing else to hand, I would use prussic acid. Do right, I say, as your art instinct commands, and take no heed of the consequences. Our function is to make the beautiful gastronomic thing, not to pander to gluttony, not to be the Jesuits of hygiene. My friend, you should see some of my compositions. At home I have books and books in manuscript, Symphonies, Picnics, Fantasies, *Etudes* . . .[3]

Yet if Wells—as these extracts suggest—found the contemporary aesthetic ideal amusing rather than inspiring, it must be remembered that *Yellow Book* aestheticism was only one element in the complex of cultural manifestations and attitudes known as the *fin de siècle*. I would claim that the young Wells, though not an aesthete, was, in essentials, a *fin de siècle* writer.

2

One of the earliest uses of the phrase in English occurs in Chapter XV of *The Picture of Dorian Gray*:

'*Fin de siècle*,' murmured Lord Henry.
'*Fin du globe*,' answered his hostess.
'I wish it were *fin du globe*,' said Dorian with a sigh. 'Life is a great disappointment.'

In its widest sense *fin de siècle* was simply the expression of a prevalent mood: the feeling that the nineteenth century—which had contained more events, more history than any other—had gone on too long, and that sensitive souls were growing weary of it. In England this mood was heightened by the feeling that Queen Victoria's reign had also lasted excessively long. But at the same time, no one knew what the coming twentieth century was going to bring, though there was no lack of speculation. The result could be described as a certain loss of nerve, weariness with the past combined with foreboding about the future. The *fin de siècle* mood produced, in turn, the feeling of *fin du globe*, the sense that the whole elaborate intellectual and social order of the nineteenth century was trembling on the brink of dissolution. *Fin de siècle* was not confined to art or aesthetics; its wider implications affected moral and social and even political attitudes and behaviour.

The fullest contemporary account of the phenomenon can be found in Max Nordau's massive work of destructive criticism, *Degeneration*. Nordau was ostensibly a scientist, a disciple of Lombroso, to whom his book is dedicated, but his tone and manner—as a contemporary reviewer observed —are rather those of the old-fashioned mad-house keeper complete with whip. Nordau's contention was that virtually all forms of late nineteenth century European art and literature—whether represented by Wagner, Ibsen, Zola, or the French symbolists—were the products of mental and physical degeneration. In his single-minded reduction of his subject to the demands of his conceptual apparatus, Nordau anticipates the rigours of twentieth century Freudian or Marxist criticism; and in general his book remains a curious but informative chapter of cultural history rather than the scientific document he intended it to be. *Degeneration* is, in fact, as much symptomatic as diagnostic: there is something decidedly *fin de siècle* about the way in which Nordau unfailingly discovers evidence of a pathological decline whenever he wants to. The English translation of *Degeneration* which appeared in 1895, was an immediate *succès de scandale* —seven impressions appeared between February and August

4

—no doubt because it coincided with the trials of Wilde. Nordau's work appeared most opportunely as the culmination of the bourgeois and philistine counter-attack against the aesthetes, which had been prepared for by the constant sniping of *Punch* throughout 1894 at Beardsley and *The Yellow Book*.[4]

The first section of *Degeneration* is entitled 'Fin de Siècle', and though characteristically intemperate in tone, it offers some useful evidence of the way in which the wider implications of the phenomenon could be regarded in the early nineties. Nordau describes its French origins—he exhibits a constant gallophobia—and shows how it has spread to Germany and other countries, though he has little to say about the English scene. He contends that the term has no objective validity, and that it illustrates a tendency of humanity to objectify its own subjective states: the French, in particular, 'ascribe their own senility to the century, and speak of *fin de siècle* when they ought correctly to say *fin de race*'. Nordau continues, in a significant passage:

But however silly a term *fin de siècle* may be, the mental constitution which it indicates is actually present in influential circles. The disposition of the times is curiously confused, a compound of feverish restlessness and blunted discouragement, of fearful presage and hang-dog renunciation. The prevalent feeling is that of imminent perdition and extinction. *Fin de siècle* is at once a confession and a complaint. The old Northern faith contained the fearsome doctrine of the Dusk of the Gods. In our days there have arisen in more highly developed minds vague qualms of a Dusk of the Nations, in which all suns and all stars are gradually waning, and mankind with all its institutions and creations is perishing in the midst of a dying world.[5]

Here Nordau is describing the *fin du globe* myth, which, as we shall see, was a dominant element in Wells's early work.

He goes on to give a list of *fin de siècle* characters or events, taken from contemporary newspapers. A king who abdicates but retains by agreement certain political rights, which he afterwards sells to his country to provide means for the liquidation of debts contracted by gambling in Paris, is a *fin de siècle* king. The police official who removes a piece of the skin of a murderer after execution and has it tanned and made into a cigar-case is a *fin de siècle* official. An American wedding ceremony held in a gasworks and the subsequent honeymoon in a balloon is a *fin de siècle* wedding. A schoolboy who, on passing the gaol where his father is imprisoned for embezzlement, remarks to a friend, 'Look, that's the governor's school,' is a *fin de siècle* son. These cases do not, at first sight, seem to have a great deal in common, but Nordau remarks:

All these *fin de siècle* cases have, nevertheless, a common feature, to wit, a contempt for traditional views of custom and morality.

Such is the notion underlying the word *fin de siècle*. It means a practical emancipation from traditional discipline, which theoretically is still in force. To the voluptuary this means unbridled lewdness, the unchaining of the beast in man; to the withered heart of the egoist, disdain of all consideration for his fellow-men, the trampling under foot of all barriers which enclose brutal greed of lucre and lust of pleasure; to the contemner of the world it means the shameless ascendency of base impulses and motives, which were, if not virtuously suppressed, at least hypocritically hidden; to the believer it means the repudiation of dogma, the negation of a super-sensuous world, the descent into flat phenomenalism; to the sensitive nature yearning for aesthetic thrills, it means the vanishing of ideals in art, and no more power in its accepted forms to arouse emotion. And to all it means the end of an established order, which for thousands of years has satisfied logic, fettered depravity, and in every art matured something of beauty.

6

One epoch of history is unmistakeably in its decline, and another is announcing its approach. There is a sound of rending in every tradition, and it is as though the morrow would not link itself with today. Things as they are totter and plunge, and they are suffered to reel and fall, because man is weary, and there is no faith that it is worth an effort to uphold them. Views that have hitherto governed minds are dead or driven hence like disenthroned kings, and for their inheritance they that hold the titles and they that would usurp are locked in struggle.[6]

If we discount the excesses of Nordau's rhetoric, we see in his analysis some of the essential elements of *fin de siècle*: the disappearance of old and familiar forms—whether in art or behaviour or intellectual attitudes—and their replacement by forms which are new and strange and even bizarre. This differs from the normal processes of development and change by being conscious and more or less *voulu*. The cult of the artificial as against the natural, which is evident *passim* in *The Picture of Dorian Gray*, is an obvious instance of this deliberate replacement, usually accompanied by an implicit or explicit desire to *épater le bourgeois*. Max Beerbohm's essay 'In Praise of Cosmetics', which appeared in the first number of *The Yellow Book*, is an ironical and urbane example, and the theme appears in much of the poetry of the period. But the most systematic abandonment of all previous forms of behaviour and modes of feeling is to be found in *A Rebours*, a work which is symptomatic of the whole *fin de siècle* state of mind, and not merely its aesthetic aspects. Des Esseintes leads a mode of life totally opposed to normal human standards; he turns night into day, abhors company, and even attempts to go without eating, being fed instead by enemas. He personifies the cult of the artificial and the unnatural far more thoroughly than Dorian Gray, his somewhat pallid imitation. He expresses the *fin de siècle* mood at its most negative, for he can only regard with blank despair the unknown manifestations of the future, as we see in the final sentences of the novel:

'Well, it is all over now. Like a tide-race, the waves of human mediocrity are rising to the heavens and will engulf this refuge, for I am opening the flood-gates myself, against my will. Ah! but my courage fails me, and my heart is sick within me!—Lord, take pity on the Christian who doubts, on the unbeliever who would fain believe, on the galley-slave of life who puts out to sea alone, in the night, beneath a firmament no longer lit by the consoling beacon-fires of the ancient hope!' [7]

3

A more positive, and perhaps more disturbing, attitude is apparent in Ibsen, who was a major target for Nordau's abuse. Bernard Shaw, in *The Quintessence of Ibsenism* (1891), described the almost hysterical hostility that greeted the early performances of Ibsen's plays in England. Throughout the nineties the bourgeois was being constantly *épaté*, by both the aesthetic and the realistic manifestations of the *fin de siècle*: following the outcry against Ibsen, comparable dismay was aroused by George Moore's *Esther Waters*, Grant Allen's *The Woman Who Did*, Beardsley's drawings, and *The Yellow Book*. With the conviction of Wilde the bourgeoisie appeared to have mounted a successful counter-attack. Yet they were still to be shocked by Hardy's *Jude the Obscure* in 1896, and in the same year Wells's *The Island of Dr Moreau* received a generally hostile reception, even though there was no suggestion of sexual impropriety in its violent pages. In Ibsen, as Shaw insisted, the likely forms of the future became painfully precise. Ibsen was that uncompromising kind of reformer who not only asserted that it was wrong to do things which no-one had previously objected to, but who also claimed that it was right to do things hitherto

8

regarded as infamous. With Ibsen we are in the realm of
the transvaluing of values, particularly where sexual morality
is concerned. Shaw claimed that just as theology and the
rule of a transcendent God had given way to rationalism
and the concept of 'duty' as a guide to conduct, so rationalism must now be replaced by the Will to Live, and duty, in
the abstract, by a man's duty to himself—or, as Ibsen had
abundantly illustrated, by a woman's duty to herself. Self-
realization was to be the paramount good, not the fulfilment
of a transcendent or altruistic morality. Ibsen, in his very
different fashion, was expressing a *fin de siècle* mood no less
than Huysmans or Wilde; his demand for moral emancipation and the untrammelled realization of the personality
was echoed, in another key, by the paradoxes of Dorian
Gray, which were themselves to acquire a tragic significance
a few years later at the Old Bailey. But, as I have said, Ibsen
was the more positive figure; many of his revolutionary
attitudes have come to form the basic assumptions of contemporary humanist morality.

However, it is to another of Nordau's victims that we
must turn in order to find the writer who can be considered
the dominant intellectual figure of the *fin de siècle*, and whose
work embodies all its various strands: Friedrich Nietzsche.
His writings had been known and discussed in Germany
through the eighties, but it was several years before they
received any attention in England. Apart from a few brief
quotations in John Davidson's *Sentences and Paragraphs* (1893)
and Nordau's denunciatory chapter in *Degeneration*, the first
sustained account of Nietzsche in English was a long essay
by Havelock Ellis published in *The Savoy* in 1896, which
concluded that 'the nineteenth century has produced no
more revolutionary and aboriginal force'. In the same year
there appeared the first two volumes of a projected English
translation of all Nietzsche's works (though the series was

not completed for several more years). These included *Thus Spake Zarathustra*, *The Twilight of the Idols*, and *The Antichrist*, works which contain most of the essential aspects of Nietzsche's thought: the 'death of God' and the transvaluing of values; the glad acceptance of the break-up of the traditional order, and the advent of the *Übermensch*. The true philosophical significance of Nietzsche's thought, whether he is a precursor of Nazism, or whether, even, he is a philosopher at all, are questions which lie far beyond the scope of this study. What is more important for my immediate purpose is to see what was made of Nietzsche's ideas when they were first received in England; Nietzsche, like Machiavelli or Freud, is one of those thinkers whose work tends to become influential at second or third hand, with all the inevitable distortions and misinterpretations that this involves. Thus, Alexander Tille, Nietzsche's first English editor, associated Nietszche with the Darwinian assertion of the primacy of struggle in the natural order. He remarked that the word 'higher' was used in two different senses with respect to the animal world and to man:

In the first case the 'higher' being among a species is that which leaves the stronger and more numerous progeny, in the latter case the 'higher' being is that which does a larger number of such acts as are believed to serve certain ends particularly esteemed by a certain portion of the community to which it belongs.[8]

For Tille, this was an unreal distinction: man was part of the animal world, and the same criteria should apply to him as to the rest of it. Tille rejected both Spencer's attempt to show that moral progress was implicit in evolutionary development, and Huxley's assertion that the cosmic process must be opposed in the interests of ethics. Tille argued that as Darwin had demonstrated the inevitability of struggle, we should adjust our values so as to admit the dominance of the 'physiological'. And this, he claimed, was precisely what Nietzsche had done: 'it is worthy of a great thinker to undertake thus the task of transvaluing the intellectual currency of our time'. Tille, it seems to me, made Nietzsche into a less complex and interesting writer than he in fact is: Nietzsche's attitude to Darwin was ambiguous and not particularly respectful, and it is not at all clear that the *Übermensch* can be identified with some ultimate product of human evolution.[9]

Nevertheless, Tille's interpretation of Nietzsche can be called plausible in its historical context, and it makes a convenient point to return to the subject of this study, the young H. G. Wells. Wells would have received the full impact of Darwin during his studies at the Royal College of Science in the late eighties, and the presence of Darwin is apparent in a number of ways in his so-called scientific romances of the next decade. Whether or not he read the English translations of Nietzsche and Tille's introduction, when they appeared in 1896, is not certain and not particularly relevant. Yet it is significant that in *The Island of Dr Moreau*, which was drafted and written the previous year, we find in the chapter called 'Dr Moreau Explains' something very like Tille's attempt to assimilate Nietzsche and Darwin. (It is interesting that in October 1896 Aubrey Beardsley, in addition to *The Island of Dr Moreau*, was also reading the new translation of Nietzsche.) In Wells's later books Nietzsche's influence may be more explicit: Ostrog, in *When the Sleeper Wakes*, claims that the coming of the 'Overman' is inevitable, while the Samurai of *A Modern Utopia*, and Wells's later versions of an élite, may be attempts to give a sociological embodiment to the *Übermensch*. Yet I am not primarily concerned with tracing influences; it is sufficient to show that both Nietzsche and Wells drew on ideas and attitudes which can, I think, be called *fin de siècle*. Both *The*

Island of Dr Moreau and *The Time Machine*, as I hope to demonstrate, make substantially the same claim as Tille in his interpretation of Nietzsche: that the traditional view of man's place in the universe, and the morality appropriate to that place, is no longer supportable.

4

The *fin du globe* motif recurs constantly in Nietzsche's work: for specific instances one may point to the section called 'Nihilism' in *The Will to Power*. And a similar preoccupation can be found in much popular literature of the time. During the final three decades of the century there appeared a large number of novels or pamphlets describing catastrophic future wars, including, in many cases, the invasion of England followed by the partial or total defeat of the nation. These works will be referred to again in Chapter V; representative examples include Sir George Chesney's *The Battle of Dorking* (1871), Sir William Butler's *The Invasion of England* (1882), William Le Quex's *The Great War in England in 1897* (1894) and F. N. Maude's *The New Battle of Dorking* (1900). In M. P. Shiel's *The Yellow Danger* (1898) we see Western civilization overrun and almost destroyed by the Chinese hordes; and in the same author's *The Purple Cloud* (1902) human society is destroyed by a natural catastrophe. It is true that many of these works were written with a homiletic purpose, to encourage the nation to a greater state of military efficiency, but this does not prevent them being, at the same time, expressions of the prevalent mood, whatever their authors' stated intentions. It was felt that the normal life of society had continued too long in its predictable and everyday fashion, and that some radical transformation was overdue, whether by war or natural disaster (in 1901 the Nietzschean magazine *The Eagle and the Serpent* published an article entitled 'Why England must be Invaded'). These novels, with their images of physical destruction, showing the fair face of England desecrated by foreign troops, afford an obvious parallel to the moral and intellectual shocks administered to bourgeois complacency and self-confidence by Ibsen and the aesthetes. Indeed, it is hard to resist the conclusion that a certain collective death-wish pervaded the national consciousness at the time, despite its superficial assertiveness and brash jingoism. The willing-ness to be shocked was at least as significant as the readiness of others to administer the shocks. As Shaw had remarked of the type of reformer who declares that it is right to do something previously regarded as infamous: 'They call him all manner of opprobrious names; grudge him his bare bread and water; and secretly adore him as their saviour from utter despair.' [10]

Nordau had complained that 'the prevalent feeling is that of imminent perdition and extinction', and this is apparent not only in the neurasthenic rejections of a des Esseintes, and the violence of the *fin du globe* novels, but in rather less ex-pected places. In Hardy's *Jude the Obscure*, published in 1896, Jude's precociously aged small son, 'Father Time', is an almost archetypal *fin de siècle* figure. When the boy has murdered Jude's other children, and killed himself, Jude observes:

It was in his nature to do it. The doctor says there are such boys springing up amongst us—boys unknown in the last generation —the outcome of new views of life. They seem to see all its terrors before they are old enough to have staying power to resist them. He says it is the beginning of the coming universal wish not to live (Part 6, Chapter 2).

Nevertheless, despite the prevalence of the negative aspects of the *fin de siècle*, they were not, in fact, universal. Just as

Nietzsche had welcomed the end of the old order and had looked for the coming of the *Übermensch*, so speculations about the future went beyond the terrors of the *fin du globe*. (As a student, Wells had taken a wholly farcical view of the possibilities of the coming era in his short story, 'A Tale of the Twentieth Century'.) Works of utopian fiction such as Edward Bellamy's *Looking Backward* (1888) and William Morris's *News from Nowhere* (1891) are important examples of the *fin de siècle* desire to discover new forms, embodied in images of a transformed society. One might also mention Richard Jefferies' *After London* (1885), a work which seems to embody the *fin du globe* motif, since it shows an England in which urban civilization has been overthrown by some unknown catastrophe, and where the whole country has reverted to a natural state (described by Jefferies in passages of great power and beauty). Yet since it also conveys Jefferies' positive conviction that human dignity is only possible in a pastoral society it can be seen as presenting a 'new form', if of a somewhat primitivistic kind. Even a war novel such as Sir William Butler's *The Invasion of England* ends on a positive and faintly utopian note: after the long years of misery and defeat, when London has almost fallen into decay, there appears 'a smaller and a cleaner city growing, as it were, amid the ruins of the old metropolis', while elsewhere the country shows healthy signs of reverting to a peasant economy. Butler, Jefferies and Morris appear agreed in their rejection of industrialism.

5

So far I have attempted to indicate, in outline, some of the intellectual components of the *fin de siècle*; they can be found equally in the writings of Nietzsche or Nordau, and in the minor imaginative works of the period, many of which have little or no literary merit. As will be seen, they dominate Wells's novels and stories of the nineties. The preoccupation with the future first appears in *The Chronic Argonauts*, a fragment of a novel Wells wrote at the age of twenty-one, and is sustained in *The Time Machine* and, less interestingly, in *When the Sleeper Wakes*. The transvaluation of values is evident in *The Island of Dr Moreau* and *The Invisible Man*, while the *fin du globe* motif is predominant in *The War of the Worlds* and several short stories. Yet, since I am concerned with Wells as an imaginative writer rather than as a purveyor of ideas, this sketch of the intellectual background of his early work must be supplemented by some account of the literary context in which it takes its place. The eighties and nineties in England were marked by an unusual variety of prose fiction. Dickens had been able more or less successfully to combine in his novels the two distinct elements of realism and romance (or fantasy). But in the final decades of the century there was an increasing tendency for the two types of fiction to assume distinct literary forms. So, on the one hand we have writers of strictly realistic fiction, such as George Moore, George Gissing and Arthur Morrison (and Wells himself, in *Love and Mr Lewisham*), and on the other many authors of fictional romances; in addition to Wilde and Stevenson, there were such secondary but immensely popular figures as Anthony Hope, Stanley Weyman and Conan Doyle. Among specific kinds of romance the ghost story was very popular, and perhaps the greatest example of the *genre* is Henry James's *Turn of the Screw*. Nordau remarked sourly on the popularity of ghost stories, and added, 'but they must come on in scientific disguise as hypnotism, telepathy, somnambulism'.[11] The classical example of the semi-supernatural, semi-scientific romance is certainly Stevenson's *Strange Case of Dr Jekyll and Mr Hyde*, which was published in 1886 and exerted

15

a considerable influence throughout the following decade, on Wells and various of his contemporaries. In the mid-nineties, at about the time Wells's first books were published, there appeared several collections of stories which made excursions into the weird and the marvellous, sometimes employing would-be scientific elements, sometimes relying on the more traditional elements of magic and the super-natural; the influence of Stevenson, and sometimes of Poe, is often evident. As examples, one may mention Arthur Machen's *The Great God Pan* (1894) and *The Three Imposters* (1895), M. P. Shiel's *Shapes in the Fire* (1896) and Vincent O'Sullivan's *A Book of Bargains* (1896). That they are now largely forgotten, whereas Wells's work in a similar vein is still read and kept in print, can, I think, be taken as a sign of his considerable literary superiority.

6

Nevertheless, Wells has not, on the whole, been taken very seriously as a literary artist; partly, perhaps, because he was at such pains in later years to deny that he was one. As one of his earliest critics, J. D. Beresford, remarked: 'The later works have been so defensive and, in one sense, didactic that one is apt to forget that many of the earlier books, and all the short stories, must have originated in the efferves-cence of creative imagination.' [12]

I want to suggest that Wells's romances are something more than the simple entertaining yarns they are generally taken to be—though without, of course, wishing to deny that they *are* admirably entertaining. I refer to them as 'romances' rather than 'scientific romances', since, apart from anything else, the adjective is not always appropriate. There are no 'scientific' elements, for instance, in a novel such as *The Wonderful Visit* or in stories like 'The Country of the

16

Blind' and 'The Door in the Wall'. Wells's early novels and tales are romances in the traditional sense, insofar as they contain an element of the marvellous, which may have a scientific—or pseudo-scientific—explanation, but which may equally originate in a supernatural happening, or in some disturbance of the individual consciousness. To stress the scientific component to the exclusion of the other qualities may give a distorted picture. It is true that Wells had had a scientific education, and frequently employed scientific language as a kind of rhetoric to ensure the plausibility of his situations; but these situations themselves may have only a tenuous, or even non-existent, connection with the actual possibilities of science. Thus, in *The Invisible Man*, Wells uses the folk-lore motif of invisibility, and apparently gives it a rational justification in terms of modern optics; never-theless, in a letter to Arnold Bennett of October 1897 he admitted the fundamental impossibility of the notion.[13] At this point one may consider the differences between Wells and Jules Verne, who is so often considered to be his pre-decessor in the manufacture of scientific romances. There can be no doubt that Wells's romances are a good deal better written than those of the excessively prolific Verne, but there is a much more fundamental difference, which Wells himself has indicated. In the preface to a collected edition of his romances, published in 1933, he wrote:

These tales have been compared with the work of Jules Verne and there was a disposition on the part of literary journalists at one time to call me the English Jules Verne. As a matter of fact there is no literary resemblance whatever between the antici-patory inventions of the great Frenchman and these fantasies. His work dealt almost always with actual possibilities of inven-tion and discovery, and he made some remarkable forecasts. The interest he invoked was a practical one; he wrote and believed and told that this or that thing could be done, which was not at that time done. He helped his reader to imagine it done and to realize what fun, excitement or mischief would ensue. Most of his inventions have 'come true'. But these stories of mine collected here do not pretend to deal with possible things; they are exercises of the imagination in a quite different field. They belong to a class of writing which includes the *Golden Ass of Apuleius*, the *True Histories of Lucian*, *Peter Schlemil*, and the story of *Frankenstein*.

As Wells insists, many of Verne's inventions have materialized since his time. Submarine travel is a commonplace, and the circumnavigation of the moon is more than a possibility. Wells's imaginings, however, remain as unattainable now as when he wrote: no one has yet contrived to travel through time, or spend several days in the Fourth Dimension of space; we are still unable to make ourselves invisible, nor can we transform animals into men by surgical means. Whereas for Verne there is a scientific element in the very conception of his story, for Wells it is merely present rhetorically. This opinion, as will be seen in Chapter VI, was shared by Verne himself, who, in old age, read certain of Wells's romances and complained of their lack of scientific foundation.

It is, I think, more helpful to compare Wells not with Verne but with such masters of the romance and the imaginative fable as Hawthorne—whose influence on his earliest work he acknowledged—or Kafka. Romance is more likely to be symbolic—even if not specifically allegorical—than realistic fiction, and this is true of Wells. Some of his critics have already hinted at the symbolic quality of his romances. V. S. Pritchett, for instance, has remarked of *The Time Machine*, 'Like all excellent works it has meanings within its meaning . . .' [14] while as long ago as 1923 Edward Shanks observed of Wells's romances, 'They are, in their degree, myths; and Mr. Wells is a myth-maker.' [15] Shanks's use of the word 'myth' is particularly suggestive; it has, of course, become a fashionable term in recent criticism, but it has a peculiar applicability to Wells's romances. The word is easier to use than to define accurately, but one can, I suggest, distinguish between major and minor myths as they occur in works of literature. The former are centred on such archetypal figures as Prometheus, Don Quixote, Faust, and Don Juan, whose significance is universal and not confined to a specific phase of cultural development (though in a sense they can be both: Faust *is* Renaissance man, but he also stands for the general human tendency towards 'over-reaching', which can occur in individuals in any kind of society and at any period). The major myths, one might say, give a generalized cultural form to certain abiding elements in the pattern of human experience. The minor myths, on the other hand, possess a wide relevance but nevertheless have a particular historical point of departure. A celebrated example is *Robinson Crusoe*, which, as Ian Watt has shown, is a myth embodying certain essential themes of modern civilization; they can be briefly described as 'Back to Nature', 'The Dignity of Labour', and 'Economic Man'.[16]

Wells's early romances are minor myths of this kind. As I have suggested, they reflect some of the dominant pre-occupations of the *fin de siècle* period; and it is important to remember that this significance is more than simply historical. If the *fin de siècle* expressed the final convulsions of the nineteenth century, it also marked the birth pangs of the twentieth, and many of the issues that concern mid-twentieth century man first appeared during that period. For that reason its literary myths still have a contemporary relevance. In *A Rebours*, for instance, we find an anticipation of the extreme eclecticism of our culture, and the rootlessness and mental and emotional fragmentation of the modern intellectual. *Dr Jekyll and Mr Hyde* vividly dramatizes the discovery of the unconscious mind, with all its revolutionary implications; we may, if we wish, go on to interpret it in Freudian terms as symbolizing the conflict between Super-ego and Id, or in a Jungian sense as illustrating the encounter between Consciousness and the Shadow.

In addition to their objective *fin de siècle* elements, Wells's romances also contain themes personal to himself, and one could, no doubt, subject them to a fairly detailed search for psychological symbolism: I have resisted the temptation to do so, except in the case of one or two short stories, where such symbolism seems unusually obtrusive. Certainly, the longer romances abound in suggestions of archetypal imagery; this is most apparent, perhaps, in *The Time Machine*, with its division between paradisal and demonic imagery, seeming to symbolize the conflict between a precarious consciousness and the increasingly menacing pressures of the unconscious. Similarly, *The Island of Dr Moreau* has various complex implications, but one can see Moreau as a manifestation of the Super-ego, eventually succumbing to the dark forces he is trying to control. Griffin, in *The Invisible Man*, has affinities with Stevenson's Dr Jekyll, and, like him, suggests the Jungian Shadow or Dark Self. *The War of the Worlds* can be read as an expression of the traditional eschatological preoccupation with the end of the world, which has been the source of so much religious imagery; equally, it expresses the myth of things or creatures falling from the skies, most recently manifested in the form of 'flying saucers'.[17]

However, my interpretation will, in general, be inclined towards history rather than psychology. Apart from certain short stories, this study will not go beyond 1901. In that year Wells published *The First Men in the Moon*, which I consider his last genuine novel-length romance, and *Anticipations*, his first major non-fictional work, where we see him ceasing to be an artist and beginning his long career as publicist and pamphleteer. It is true that the following year there appeared *The Sea Lady*, which can be considered a romance; but though it is a *jeu d'esprit* of some charm it is, I think, essentially an expression of certain recurring themes in Wells's realistic fiction, which had first appeared in *Love and Mr Lewisham*, and were to be more fully explored in *The New Machiavelli* and later novels. While the early romances originated in what J. D. Beresford called 'the effervescence of creative imagination', Wells's later attempts at the form all had a didactic aim, and suffered an according loss of imaginative power. They are no longer myths, merely illustrations of an argument. This is true of *The Food of the Gods* (1904); although the first part of the book contains a good deal of Wells's customary imaginative exuberance, his homiletic purpose becomes fatally obtrusive in the later chapters (Wells remarked in his autobiography that the novel was based on a Fabian paper called *The Question of Scientific Administrative Areas*).[18] And this applies still more to such later works as *In the Days of the Comet* (1906), *The World Set Free* (1914), *Men Like Gods* (1923) and *The Dream* (1924).

The War in the Air (1908) is a rather different case. It is less immediately didactic than these works, and correspondingly more entertaining. Its hero, the ebullient Bert Smallways, has a recognizable affinity with the heroes of Wells's realistic fiction, such as Kipps or Mr Polly. Insofar as it is a romance, it is of a more strictly 'scientific' kind, in the Verne sense, than any of Wells's works of the nineties. It is partly a vivid prophecy of the military possibilities of aeronautics, and partly an apocalyptic reflection on the growing likelihood of a major war, inspired by the increasing power of Imperial Germany. In some ways it is a return to Wells's *fin du globe* note of the nineties, and is a by no means negligible work, but it lacks the depth and complexity of the earlier romances.

Wells, at the beginning of his career, was a genuine and original imaginative artist, who wrote several books of considerable literary importance, before dissipating his talents in directions which now seem more or less irrelevant. In considering these works, it will be necessary to modify the customary view of Wells as an optimist, a utopian and a passionate believer in human progress. The dominant note of his early years was rather a kind of fatalistic pessimism, combined with intellectual scepticism, and it is this which the early romances reflect. It is, one need hardly add, a typically *fin de siècle* note.

CHAPTER II

FROM 'THE CHRONIC ARGONAUTS' TO
'THE TIME MACHINE'

I

WELLS's personal and literary career up to 1895 was ade-
quately and succinctly summed up in a letter written in that
year to Grant Richards. (Richards had accepted a short
story by Wells, 'The Argonauts of the Air', for *Phil May's
Annual*, and had asked the author for some facts about
himself):

Nov. 6/95.

MY DEAR SIR,

It's awfully good of you to go writing up a reputation for me,
and I very gladly do what you ask of me. I was born at a place
called Bromley in Kent, a suburb of the damnedest, in 1866,
educated at a beastly little private school there until I was thirteen,
apprenticed on trial to all sorts of trades, attracted the attention
of a man called Byatt, Headmaster of Midhurst Grammar School,
by the energy with which I mopped up Latin—I went to him
for Latin for a necessary examination while apprenticed (on
approval, of course!) to a chemist there, became a kind of teaching scholar to him, got a scholarship at the Royal College of
Science, S. Kensington (1884), worked there three years, started
a students' journal, read abundantly in the Dyce and Foster
Library, failed my last year's examination (geology), wandered
in the wilderness of private school teaching, had a lung haemorrhage, got a London degree B.Sc. (1889) with first and second-
class honours, private coaching, *Globe* turnovers, article in the
Fortnightly (1890),[1] edited an obscure educational paper, had

haemorrhage for the second time (1893), chucked coaching and went for journalism. *P.M.G.* took up my work, then Henley (*N.Obs.*). Hind *P.M. Budget* set me on to short stories. Found *Saturday Review* when Harris bought the paper. *Review of Reviews* first paper to make a fuss over *Time Machine*—for which I shall never cease to be grateful. *Referee*, next. Brings me up to date.

> Books published:
> Text Book of Biology. A cram book—and pure hackwork. (Illustrations grotesquely bad—facts imagined.)
> Time Machine
> Wonderful Visit
> Stolen Bacillus
>   Forthcoming:—
> The Island of Dr Moreau. Jan 1896.

I am dropping all journalism now, and barring a few short stories to keep the wolf from the door am concentrating upon two long stories—one of these is a cycling romance (I am a cyclist), the other a big scientific story remotely resembling the *Time Machine*. I am trying to secure a serial publication of these in 1896—if ever I get them finished.

But this is enough of facts. Use any you fancy and believe me
Always yours very sincerely,
H. G. WELLS.[2]

Whilst still a schoolboy at Bromley Wells was engaged in vigorous literary activity, and the manuscript of a story that he wrote and illustrated at the age of twelve has recently been published in facsimile in America.[3] During the years of apprenticeship and hard struggle in his teens he continued to write whenever he had an opportunity, and Geoffrey West records that at seventeen Wells wrote two stories; one was called 'Potted Onions' and the other described the adventures of Otto Noxious, 'explorer and Munchausen'.[4]

But Wells's main stimulus to literary creation came during his years as a student at the Royal College of Science. He helped to found the students' magazine, the *Science Schools Journal*, and was editor of the first few issues. Between 1886 and 1890 he contributed a large number of stories and essays to this magazine under a variety of pseudonyms.[5] In 1887, soon after he left the College, Wells had a short story accepted by the *Family Herald* and began work on a novel called *Lady Frankland's Companion*, which he subsequently destroyed.[6] Some months later, while recovering from a breakdown in health, he wrote the fragment of a fantastic novel called *The Chronic Argonauts* which is the most ambitious and important piece of writing surviving from his earliest years. It was serialized in the *Science Schools Journal* in April, May and June 1888, and was never completed. This work was, in effect, the first draft of *The Time Machine*, though the differences between the two works are much more apparent than the resemblances.

2

In his autobiography Wells wrote of *The Chronic Argonauts*:

Moreover, I began a romance, very much under the influence of Hawthorne, which was printed in the *Science Schools Journal*, the *Chronic Argonauts*. I broke this off after three instalments because I could not go on with it. That I realized I could not go on with it marks a stage in my education in the art of fiction. It was the original draft of what later became the *Time Machine*, which first won me recognition as an imaginative writer.[7]

There is no question that the story is an immature piece of writing, and the kind of work that an established author would find an embarrassment in his later years, but it possesses considerable narrative powers and it would not be difficult to predict, on the strength of *The Chronic Argonauts*, that its author might go on to do much better work in the future. The decidedly leisurely manner of the beginning of the story makes it clear that Wells envisaged it as having the dimensions of a novel, though in the event only about ten thousand words were completed and published. The story is set in Wales, in and around the Carnarvonshire village of Llyddwdd, and one may assume that some, at least, of the details of the setting were recalled from Wells's brief period as a schoolmaster in Wales in the summer of 1887. There is an old house near the village, the Manse, which is said to be haunted by the ghost of an old man named Williams, who had been murdered there by his two sons many years before. Interest is aroused by the mysterious arrival of a stranger who takes up residence in the Manse and soon provokes both extreme curiosity and hostility among the villagers by his strange activities and surly and uncommunicative manner. His name, it is learned, is Dr Moses Nebogipfel, Ph.D., F.R.S. He is described as:

a small-bodied, sallow faced little man, clad in a close-fitting garment of some stiff, dark material, which Mr Parry Davies, the Llyddwdd shoemaker, opined was leather. His aquiline nose, thin lips, high cheek-ridges, and pointed chin, were all small and mutually well-proportioned; but the bones and muscles of his face were rendered excessively prominent and distinct by his extreme leanness. The same cause contributed to the sunken appearance of the large eager-looking grey eyes, that gazed forth from under his phenomenally wide and high forehead. It was this latter feature that most powerfully attracted the attention of an observer. It seemed to be great beyond all preconceived ratio to the rest of his countenance. Dimensions, corrugations, wrinkles, venation, were alike abnormally exaggerated. Below it his eyes glowed like lights, in some cave at a cliff's foot. It so overpowered and suppressed the rest of his face as to give an *unhuman* appearance almost, to what would otherwise have been an unquestionably handsome profile. The lank black hair that hung unkempt before his eyes served to increase rather than conceal this effect, by adding to unnatural altitude a suggestion of hydrocephalic projection: and the idea of something ultra human was furthermore accentuated by the temporal arteries that pulsated visibly through his transparent yellow skin.

The villagers' superstitious fear of Nebogipfel is brought to a head when a village hunchback drops dead in a fit: they become convinced that he had been bewitched by 'the warlock', and an angry mob marches with torches to the Manse. The vicar, the Rev. Elijah Ulysses Cook, goes in advance to warn Nebogipfel. The first instalment of the story ends with the mob of villagers bursting into the Manse and finding Nebogipfel and Cook standing together on a mechanical contraption; an instant later, the two men vanish.

The second instalment suggests that Wells was experimenting rather wildly with narrative methods. It does not open in Llyddwdd, but somewhere in Fenland, where 'the author' is lying in thought by the edge of a lake. A strange machine carrying two men suddenly appears on an island in the lake. It quickly disappears again, but not before one of the men, a clergyman, has been left behind. 'The author' punts across to the island, finds the clergyman in a bad way, and takes him back to his house, where he remains insensible for ten days. It is learnt that he is the Rev. Elijah Cook, who had disappeared from Llyddwdd with Dr Nebogipfel some three weeks before. When he has somewhat recovered he tells the author that he has a deposition to make concerning the murder of an old man named Williams in 1862, 'the abduction of a ward in the year 4003', 'several assaults on public officials in the years 17901 and 2' and 'valuable medical, social, and physiographical data for all time'. The deposition is taken down, and soon afterwards the clergyman dies.

The next section of the story gives the clergyman's deposition. It describes how, when Cook goes into the Manse at Llyddwdd to warn Nebogipfel, he finds it littered with diagrams and strange mechanical apparatus. Nebogipfel is absent, but an instant later he is startled by the sudden noiseless appearance of the doctor, 'ghastly pale, with red stained hands, crouching upon a strange-looking metallic platform, and with his deep grey eyes looking intently into the visitor's face'. The platform, Cook observes, is also stained with blood, and a moment later he faints. When he recovers he finds Dr Nebogipfel, no longer blood-stained, kneeling by him, offering him a glass of brandy. The doctor then explains that his apparatus is called 'the Chronic Argo', and that it is a machine by which he can travel through time. He gives a highly romantic account of himself, saying that he has always resembled the Ugly Duckling in Hans Andersen's story:

'That story, if you understand it well, will tell you almost all that you should know of me to comprehend how that machine came to be thought of in a mortal brain . . . Even when I read that simple narrative for the first time, a thousand bitter experiences had begun the teaching of my isolation among the people of my birth,—I knew the story was for me. The ugly duckling that proved to be a swan, that lived through all contempt and bitterness, to float at last sublime. From that hour forth, I dreamt of meeting with my kind, dreamt of encountering that sympathy I knew was my profoundest need. Twenty years I lived in that hope, lived and worked, lived and wandered, loved even, and, at last, despaired.'

He continues:

'In short, Mr Cook, I discovered that I was one of those superior Cagots called a genius—a man born out of my time—a

man thinking the thoughts of a wiser age, doing things and believing things that men now *cannot* understand, and that in the
years ordained to me there was nothing but silence and suffering
for my soul—unbroken solitude, man's bitterest pain. I knew I
was an Anachronic Man; my age was still to come. One filmy
hope alone held me to life, a hope to which I clung until it had
become a certain thing. Thirty years of unremitting toil and
deepest thought among the hidden things of matter and form and
life, and then *that*, the Chronic Argo, *the ship that sails through
time*, and now I go to join my generation, to journey through
the ages till my time has come.'

After this confession by Nebogipfel, he and Cook discuss
the principles of 'time travelling', about which the latter is
inclined to be sceptical. Nebogipfel admits that the notion
not only jars with accepted opinions but 'defies accepted
opinions to mortal combat'. He goes on to assert that
opinions of any kind, 'Scientific Theories, Laws, Articles of
Belief . . . Logical Premises, Ideas', are all necessarily 'diagrammatic caricatures of the ineffable' with no reality in
themselves, and only to be used where they are 'necessary in
the shaping of results—as chalk outlines are necessary to the
painter and plans and sections to the engineer'. Here we
have an anticipation of the extreme nominalist position that
Wells was to expound in the first article he published in a
national magazine, the quasi-philosophical paper called
'The Rediscovery of the Unique', which appeared in the
Fortnightly Review for July 1891. This nominalism, though
originally held in a very uninformed way, was to remain a
basic intellectual attitude with Wells throughout his life.

Nebogipfel continues his 'explanation' by saying that
most people believe in the *reality* of traditional geometrical
conceptions, even though they are patently inadequate. A
cube, for instance, to exist in reality must possess not only
the three dimensions of space, but a fourth dimension of

duration or time as well. But once the possibility of this 'fourth dimension' is allowed for, 'Locomotion along lines of duration—chronic navigation comes within the range first of geometrical theory, and then of practical mechanics'. The clergyman is gradually becoming convinced when he remembers the blood he had seen on Nebogipfel's hands. The latter explains that he had travelled back in time to the point when the Manse had been occupied by old Williams and his sons. He appeared in the room, and the old man had sprung at him, thinking he was the Devil, and Nebogipfel had killed him in self-defence. At this point the two men hear the mob outside sweeping up to the Manse, crying 'Burn the warlock! Burn the murderer!' and a moment later the angry crowd burst into the room. Nebogipfel drags Cook to the Chronic Argo, and with 'a thunderous roar like the bursting forth of a great fountain of water' it begins its voyage. Here the story breaks off, though it is manifestly incomplete. Wells appended a brief note:

How did it end? How came it that Cook wept with joy to return once more to this nineteenth century of ours? Why did not Nebogipfel remain with him? All that, and more also, has been written, and will or will never be read, according as Fate may have decreed to the Curious Reader.

As we have seen, Wells considered that the work was written largely under the influence of Hawthorne, and he went on to remark, 'there is a lot of fuss about the hostility of a superstitious Welsh village from Hawthorne's *Scarlet Letter*'.[8] In fact, one may doubt whether *The Scarlet Letter* was so specific an influence on *The Chronic Argonauts* as this suggests, for the resemblances between Wells's story and Hawthorne's romance are scarcely pronounced, beyond a certain similarity of atmosphere. If anything, the mass hysteria of the villagers and the legacy of murder seem to owe more to the opening pages of *The House of the Seven Gables*. Nevertheless, the mere fact of Wells's acknowledging the influence of Hawthorne on his earliest fiction is significant, since it puts him into a direct relation with a major nineteenth-century writer of symbolic fiction. In addition to Hawthorne, Wells's youthful imagination had been nurtured on fictional romance, for at the age of fourteen or so he was enjoying Eugene Sue's *Mysteries of Paris*, *Vathek*, *Rasselas*, and *Gulliver's Travels*.[9] These influences had been absorbed long before his encounter with the intellectual world of South Kensington.

Yet though *The Chronic Argonauts* is very much a traditional romance, it does contain the seeds of the 'scientific' notion on which *The Time Machine* was to depend, the idea of 'time travelling', and the only passages where the two works at all resemble each other are in the accounts of the principles of time travelling. In 1903 Wells wrote of *The Time Machine*, 'The idea of this book was first evolved in the Debating Society of these schools'[10] (i.e. of the Royal College of Science), and the specific occasion when the idea first presented itself to Wells may have been a debate held on 14 January 1887, when a student named E. A. Hamilton-Gordon read a paper on the 'Fourth Dimension'. This paper was printed in the April 1887 issue of the *Science Schools Journal*, though unfortunately a report of the debate was not included. But Wells was a keen member of the society and there is every reason to suppose that he was present and joined in the discussion. Hamilton-Gordon's paper is a rather obscurely written but basically straightforward account of the possibilities of multidimensional non-Euclidean geometries: he attempts to show that in theory it is perfectly possible to invent and describe objects existing in four-dimensional space which would bear the same relation to a cube as the latter does to a plane square. Such a figure, which can be described but not represented visually, seems to be a commonplace to modern mathematicians; but in the eighties, it appears, the notion was still original and unfamiliar. Hamilton-Gordon's paper makes it clear that the term 'Fourth Dimension' was applied to several different things:

The question has been put to me with monotonous frequency, 'What is the fourth dimension?' and it would be difficult to answer, were it not for the fact that the questioner usually answers it for himself, by suggesting some impossible thing. One thought it was 'Time', another 'Life', a third 'Heaven', while a fourth suggested 'Velocity'.[11]

The first alternative mentioned, 'Time', is—as Nebogipfel's explanation showed—an equal claimant for the name of 'fourth dimension', since some degree of duration is necessary to all material objects, even though 'locomotion along lines of duration' does not necessarily become possible. Discussions about the 'Fourth Dimension' seem to have been in the air in the eighties, for at the end of his paper Hamilton-Gordon added the following note:

Since writing the above, a pamphlet has been put into my hands entitled, 'What is the Fourth Dimension', and to my disgust I find it is an almost exact counterpart of my theory, which I had imagined to be new and original. However, since the pamphlet bears the date of publication, 1887, and the lines of this paper were drawn up in 1886, the sin of purloining cannot be laid at my door.[12]

The pamphlet in question was probably C. H. Hinton's *What is the Fourth Dimension?*, which had first appeared in 1884. This was the first of Hinton's series of 'Scientific Romances', which appeared at intervals throughout the eighties and nineties and popularized various scientific facts and possibilities. Oscar Wilde may well have been aware of Hinton's pamphlet, or some similar contemporary discussion, for in his story 'The Canterville Ghost', he says of the Ghost, 'There was evidently no time to be lost, so, hastily adopting the Fourth Dimension of Space as a means of escape, he vanished through the wainscoting, and the house became quite quiet.'[13]

Both concepts of the Fourth Dimension—as a further dimension of space, and as duration of time—offered a good deal of scope to the writer of scientific romance, and Wells made use of both of them. In *The Chronic Argonauts* and *The Time Machine* he is concerned with the Fourth Dimension as time, though in the latter work he also shows himself aware of the alternative view, and refers to the work of the distinguished American mathematician, Professor Simon Newcomb. Though time travelling, as expounded by Nebogipfel, and later by the hero of *The Time Machine*, was the imaginative product of serious discussion about multidimensional geometries, it is an essentially pseudo-scientific notion, despite the immensely plausible way in which Wells treats the topic in *The Time Machine*. Van Wyck Brooks, writing in 1915, said that he was unable to see what was wrong with the exposition of time travelling,[14] but other writers had already pointed out the logical impossibility of travelling in time. Within a few months of the appearance of *The Time Machine* in 1895, Israel Zangwill had discussed at some length in a review the impossibility of the book's basic idea,[15] and a more systematic refutation was given in philosophical language in 1914 by W. B. Pitkin.[16] However, such demonstrations of the scientific impossibility of the book's underlying concept in no way detract from the imaginative quality and mythical power of *The Time Machine*.

The concept of the Fourth Dimension as a form of non-Euclidean space also introduces certain interesting imaginative possibilities, since one can posit a number of self-contained three-dimensional worlds existing, as it were, side by side in four-dimensional space, but with no direct contact between them. One can then imagine beings transferred from one such world to another by passing them through the Fourth Dimension, as one might transfer objects from one enclosed plane surface to another by lifting them and so passing them through a third dimension. Wells was to make use of this possibility in his second novel, *The Wonderful Visit* and in the tale called 'The Plattner Story', and was to return to it in a much later novel, *Men Like Gods* (1923).

However, fascinating though these geometrical speculations may be, they are only incidental to the central interest of *The Chronic Argonauts* and *The Time Machine*. As I have said, Wells's imagination was conditioned to romance before he knew very much about science, and the central figure of *The Chronic Argonauts*, Dr Nebogipfel, though supposedly a scientist and F.R.S., is a strange character to have been produced by the keen young student who had studied under Huxley. In fact, he has very little to do with the atmosphere of progressive thinking and intellectual inquiry that had characterized the Royal College of Science in the eighties (an atmosphere well conveyed in Wells's story 'A Slip Under the Microscope' and his novel, *Love and Mr Lewisham*), and a great deal to do with a literary tradition exemplified by Mary Shelley's Frankenstein and Stevenson's Dr Jekyll. Stevenson's story had appeared in 1886, two years before Wells's romance. Nebogipfel is the scientist as magician or alchemist, rather than the sober investigator of the physical world, and substantially the same type is to recur in Wells's fiction as Dr Moreau, and Griffin, the Invisible Man. Nebogipfel, like Frankenstein, is of a solitary and secretive disposition. To this extent, too, he corresponds to the contemporary aesthetic ideal of the artist who must necessarily be isolated and suffering before he can create.[17] But if Frankenstein represented a type of solitary romantic hero (a type monstrously caricatured in his creation, who eventually destroys his master), Nebogipfel is more than this, for he is not only not of his own time, but specifically of a future time: 'a man born out of my time— a man thinking the thoughts of a wiser age, doing things and believing things that men now *cannot* understand. . . .' Thus, Nebogipfel embodies an image of the future, and such images were by no means uncommon in writers of the eighties and nineties, who tended to be a good deal taken up with hopes and fears about the coming century: Max Nordau was to stigmatize a preoccupation with the future as symptomatic of the *fin de siècle* mentality.

Nebogipfel is not only a man of the future; he also refers to himself as 'an ugly duckling', isolated among his fellow men, and it is not difficult to associate this remark with the young Wells's own feelings about himself. He would certainly have felt, during the unhappy years as a drapers' apprentice in his teens, that 'a thousand bitter experiences had begun the teaching of my isolation among the people of my birth', and that his hope could only lie in the future. Nebogipfel, as an exile from the future, sees it as a Promised Land, and here we have the significance of his name, *Moses Nebo-Gipfel*. Wells subsequently showed himself aware of this symbolic intention, but dismissed it:

And the story is clumsily invented, and loaded with irrelevant sham significance. The time traveller, for example, is called Nebo-gipfel, though manifestly Mount Nebo had no business whatever in that history. There was no Promised Land ahead.[18]

Wells was simply being imperceptive here, for the point is made clearly enough in Nebogipfel's explanation of the principles of time-travelling: 'And now another step, and the hidden past and unknown future are before us. We stand upon a mountain summit with the plains of the ages spread below.' Like Dickens and Henry James, Wells sometimes gave his characters names of a symbolic nature.

In thematic terms there is more to *The Chronic Argonauts* than either a merely fashionable speculation about the future, or an expression of the young Wells's isolation and dissatisfaction with his environment. In one sense it *is*, even though obliquely, a product of Wells's scientific training, for it represents an imaginative reaction to evolution, not in respect of man's past but of his possible future development. Nebogipfel, the man of the future, with his strange bulging forehead, who appears both 'unhuman' and 'ultra human', is an image—admittedly romantic rather than scientific—of the possible future condition of humanity. It was a theme which was to occupy Wells throughout his life, and his first systematic treatment of it was in a paper called 'The Past and Future of the Human Race', delivered to the College Debating Society in 1885, though the earliest surviving version was published in the *Pall Mall Budget* on 16 November 1893 under the title of 'The Man of the Year Million'.[19] A revised version of this article with the title 'Of a Book Unwritten', was subsequently included in Wells's book of essays, *Certain Personal Matters*. Here Wells observes:

. . . primitive man in the works of the descriptive anthropologist, is certainly a very entertaining and quaint person, but the man of the future, if we only had the facts, would appeal to us more strongly. Yet where are the books? As Ruskin has said somewhere, *apropos* of Darwin, it is not what man has been but what he will be, that should interest us.[20]

Wells's 'man of the year million' has enormously increased in mental capacity and has correspondingly declined in physical development, with the exception of his hands, which are still of use to him:

Eyes large, lustrous, beautiful, soulful: above them, no longer separated by rugged brow ridges, is the top of the head, a glistening, hairless dome, terete and beautiful; no craggy nose rises to disturb by its unmeaning shadows the symmetry of that calm face, no vestigial ears project; the mouth is a small, perfectly round aperture, toothless and gumless, jawless, unanimal, no futile emotions disturbing its roundness as it lies, like the harvest moon or the evening star, in the wide firmament of face.[21]

He will no longer eat and digest food as he does now, but will nourish himself 'in elegant simplicity by immersion in a tub of nutritive fluid'.

Watch them as they hop on their hands—a method of progression advocated by Bjornsen—about the pure white marble floor. Great hands they have, enormous brains, soft, liquid, soulful eyes. Their whole muscular system, their legs, their abdomens, are shrivelled to nothing, a dangling, degraded pendant to their minds.[22]

'The Man of the Year Million' is, with *The Chronic Argonauts*, the most important piece of published work surviving from Wells's South Kensington days. After it had appeared in the *Pall Mall Budget* it was caricatured with a satirical poem in *Punch*.[23] Wells's speculation was evidently found disturbing, and not least disturbing was the carefully ambiguous tone of the piece, for it is impossible to tell whether Wells is horrified by or secretly rather approving of what he describes: the general effect is of an extremely ironic detachment. This ambiguity of tone is characteristic of much of his early writing and, I think, conceals a basic uncertainty of personal attitude. But the major interest of 'The Man of the Year Million' lies in its theme, the possibility of human evolutionary development, which Wells was to return to frequently in his later fiction. He does, in fact, make the following ironical reference to it in *The War of the Worlds*:

It is worthy of remark that a certain speculative writer of quasi-scientific repute, writing long before the Martian invasion, did forecast for man a final structure not unlike the actual Martian condition. His prophecy, I remember, appeared in November or December, 1893, in a long defunct publication, the *Pall Mall Budget*, and I recall a caricature of it in a pre-Martian periodical called *Punch* (II. 2).

The War of the Worlds is one of several books partially inspired by the impact of Darwin, but the most complete account of the possible development of man into something both 'unhuman' and 'ultra human' is to be found in *The Time Machine*.

3

Although *The Chronic Argonauts* was never completed, Wells continued to be interested in the story, and between 1889 and 1892 he made two more versions of it. They have not survived, but Geoffrey West quotes an account given of them by A. Morley Davies, a college friend of Wells's:

In the first rewriting Dr Nebogipfel and the Rev. Elijah Ulysses Cook still appear, but the scene shifts to a village on the South Downs. They arrive in a future much less changed from our time than that portrayed in *The Time Machine*. The upper and lower worlds exist, but their inhabitants are not yet two distinct species. A scientific aristocracy still survives in a decadent form as a red-robed priesthood, and art and literature are cultivated in a very dilettante manner. The Chronic Argonauts stir up these weary idlers, and even make it fashionable to read books. The priests take their visitors to see a vast museum, but themselves grow bored and leave the pair to explore alone, warning them against the passages which lead 'down'. They go 'down', and discover an underworld working to support the upper world. Eventually some compunction is aroused among the aristocracy, and some kindly disposed persons descend to sing and play to the workers. At this the underworld explodes into revolution, kills them, and rushes up in a mob to carry out a general massacre. In the ensuing panic the argonauts make for their machine. Cook has become fascinated by a certain Lady Dis, and tries to take her with him, but in the excitement of the escape he discovers that all her beauty is artificial and flings her off as he climbs into the machine. They travel back to our own time, but overshoot the mark and are nearly killed by a party of palaeolithic men. At last they hit the nineteenth century, when Nebogipfel drops Cook and then vanishes with the machine.

In the third version, of which fragments only were read to me, Nebogipfel and Cook are cut out. There is no such underworld as in the earlier version and *The Time Machine*, the future being one in which a ruling class governs by hypnotism, but the end of the story is somewhat similar to that given above. One of the priests determines to put an end to the hypnotism and calls to the people to awake. They awake and kill him, and march with his head on a pole to slay his fellows. In the panic the same revelation is made of the artificial means by which the ruling class had hidden the physical degeneration resulting from their idle life. This third version never pleased me, and I was glad when *The Time Machine* went back to something nearer the original idea.[24]

The next version of the story was made in 1894. Since the middle of the previous year Wells had been living by free-lance journalism, contributing mainly to the *Pall Mall Gazette*: many of these articles were subsequently collected in his two books of essays, *Select Conversations with an Uncle* (1895), and *Certain Personal Matters* (1897). Early in 1894 he was introduced to W. E. Henley, then editing the *National Observer*, who invited him to contribute to the paper. Wells responded to the invitation by returning to the theme of 'time travelling', and in March of that year we find him writing to A. M. Davies:

I have also responded to an invitation by the *National Observer* and that old corpse of the Chronic Argo is being cut up into articles one last Saturday (Time Travelling) one next number and possibly others to follow.[25]

As will be apparent from this reference, Wells had undertaken to contribute a series of separate articles on the theme of time travelling rather than a sustained narrative. Nevertheless, these articles are much closer to *The Time Machine* in its finished state than the earlier versions, though they contain only a fraction of the material. Seven articles were published, unsigned, in the *National Observer* between March and June 1894, and then the series was broken off, probably because Henley had given up the editorship. During the summer Wells continued to work at the story, though without immediate hope of publication. In a letter to his father, dated 10 August 1894, he remarked, 'I have been writing a longer thing on spec.'[26] But at the end of the year Henley took over the editorship of the monthly *New Review*, with William Heinemann as publisher. Henley at once accepted the finished *Time Machine* as a serial story, and it appeared in five instalments between January and May 1895. In May the novel was published as a book by Heinemann, and an edition appeared in New York from Henry Holt and Co. at about the same time.[27]

Wells was conscious that *The Time Machine* was his most ambitious work so far, and in December 1894 he wrote to his friend Elizabeth Healey:

You may be interested to know that our ancient *Chronic Argonauts* of the *Science Schools Journal* has at last become a complete story and will appear as a serial in the *New Review* for January. It's my trump card and if it does not come off very much I shall know my place for the rest of my career.[28]

Wells did not have long to wait for an assurance of the success of the story, for a notice in the March number of the influential *Review of Reviews* praised it in the highest terms: 'Mr H. G. Wells, who is writing the serial in the *New Review*, is a man of genius.' [29] Similar laudatory remarks were made in the April and May numbers,[30] and apparently the author was the editor of the *Review of Reviews* himself, W. T. Stead, even though Stead was no friend of Henley and his enterprises. Grant Richards, at that time assistant editor, took the credit for having first brought the story to Stead's notice, and claimed that he may even have written the original notice himself, though other authorities ascribe it to Stead.[31] Stead returned to Wells's praise three years later, in a long review-article on *The War of the Worlds*, which he made the occasion of a retrospective survey of Wells's works to date.[32]

The novel was published in a cheap edition, in ten thousand copies. It was not widely reviewed, but those reviews that did appear tended to be very favourable. The *Daily Chronicle*, for instance, wrote of it:

No two books could be more unlike than 'The Time Machine' and 'The Strange Case of Dr Jekyll and Mr Hyde', but since the appearance of Stevenson's creepy romance we have had nothing in the domain of pure fantasy so bizarre as this 'invention' by Mr H. G. Wells. For his central idea Mr Wells may be indebted to some previously unpublished narrative suggestion, but if so we must confess ourselves entirely unacquainted with it, and so far as our knowledge goes he has produced that rarity which Solomon declared to be not merely rare but non-existent—a 'new thing under the sun'.[33]

In August 1895 the monthly *Bookman* published a note on Wells, complete with portrait.[34] The foundations of his literary career had been firmly laid.

The Time Machine has continued to be popular, though it

has never, so far as I know, been given a sustained critical examination. V. S. Pritchett, one of the best of Wells's modern critics, has said of it, in a passage already referred to:

Without question *The Time Machine* is the best piece of writing. It will take its place among the great stories of our language. Like all excellent works it has meanings within its meaning . . .[35]

One may compare Edward Shanks's earlier observation:

If I were to say that many of Mr Wells's early books have a poetic quality I should run the risk of conveying a false impression. Luckily they have a peculiar quality which enables them to bear a special description. They are, in their degree, myths; and Mr Wells is a myth-maker.[36]

Shanks expended his remarks with particular reference to *The Island of Dr Moreau*, though they apply equally to *The Time Machine*:

These passages suggest one interpretation of the book. But it is a myth, not an allegory; and, whereas an allegory bears a single and definite interpretation, a myth does not, but can be interpreted in many ways, none of them quite consistent, all of them more alive and fruitful than the rigid allegorical correspondence.[37]

Pritchett has in fact referred to *The Time Machine* as a 'poetic social allegory'. But this narrows the effective range of the work too much; though on one level the 'allegory', or in Shanks's more appropriate term, the 'myth', does operate in social terms, its further significance is biological and even cosmological. But in any event, the work's mythical implications are only possible because of the primary excellence of its structural and narrative qualities.

Structurally, *The Time Machine* belongs to the class of story, which includes James's *Turn of the Screw* and Conrad's *Lord Jim*, that Northrop Frye has called 'the tale told in quotation marks, where we have an opening setting with a small group of congenial people, and then the real story told by one of the members'. As Frye observes:

The effect of such devices is to present the story through a relaxed and contemplative haze as something that entertains us without, so to speak, confronting us, as direct tragedy confronts us.[38]

This aesthetic distancing of the central narrative of *The Time Machine*, 'the time traveller's story', is carefully carried out. At the end of the book, the Traveller says:

'No, I cannot expect you to believe it. Take it as a lie—or a prophecy. Say I dreamed it in the workshop. Consider I have been speculating upon the destinies of our race, until I have hatched this fiction. Treat my assertion of its truth as a mere stroke of art to enhance its interest. And taking it as a story, what do you think of it?' (16).

The manifest disbelief of all his friends (with the exception of the story-teller)—one of them 'thought the tale a "gaudy lie" ' (16)—is balanced by the apparent evidence of his sojourn in the future, the 'two strange white flowers' of an unknown species. In fact Wells demands assent by apparently discouraging it, a device he was frequently to use in his fantastic short stories.

The opening chapters of the novel show us the inventor entertaining his friends, a group of professional men, in the solid comfort of his home at Richmond. They clearly derive from the 'club-man' atmosphere with which several of Kipling's short stories open, and their function in the narrative is to give it a basis in contemporary life at its most ordinary and pedestrian: this atmosphere makes the completest possible contrast with the tale that is to come, with its account of a wholly imaginative world of dominantly paradisal and demonic imagery, lying far outside the possible experience of the late Victorian bourgeoisie. These chapters are essential to Wells's purpose, since they prevent the central narrative from seeming a piece of pure fantasy, or a fairy story, and no more. The character of the Time Traveller himself—cheerful, erratic, and somewhat absurd, faintly suggestive of a hero of Jerome K. Jerome's—has a similar function. One may compare the work of other popular writers of fantastic romance in the nineties, such as Arthur Machen and M. P. Shiel (both deriving from Stevenson), where a 'weird' atmosphere is striven after from the very beginning and the dramatic power is correspondingly less. Wells was conscious of this technique; in a magazine interview he gave in 1897 he admitted that though there was a distinction in his own work between 'realism' and 'romance', the two could never be wholly separate, since 'the scientific episode which I am treating insists upon interesting me, and so I have to write about the effect of it upon the mind of some particular person'.[39]

Once the reader has been initiated into the group of friends, he is prepared for whatever is to come next. First the model time machine is produced—'a glittering metallic framework, scarcely larger than a small clock, and very delicately made . . . there was ivory in it, and some crystalline substance' (12)—and sent off into time, never to be seen again. Then we are shown the full-scale machine, and the account of it is a brilliant example of Wells's impressionistic method:

I remember vividly the flickering light, his queer, broad head in silhouette, the dance of the shadows, how we all followed him, puzzled but incredulous, and how there in the laboratory we beheld a larger edition of the little mechanism which we had seen vanish from before our eyes. Parts were of nickel, parts of ivory, parts had certainly been filed or sawn out of rock crystal. The thing was generally complete, but the twisted crystalline bars lay unfinished upon the bench beside some sheets of drawings, and I took one up for a better look at it. Quartz it seemed to be (2).

One sees here how much Wells's narrative technique had developed since the days of *The Chronic Argonauts*. The assemblage of details is strictly speaking meaningless but nevertheless conveys very effectively a sense of the machine without putting the author to the taxing necessity of giving a direct description. As a reviewer of one of his later books was to remark, 'Precision in the unessential and vagueness in the essential are really the basis of Mr Wells's art, and convey admirably the just amount of conviction.'[40]

The central narrative of *The Time Machine* is of a kind common to several of Wells's early romances; a character is transferred to or marooned in a wholly alien environment, and the story arises from his efforts to deal with the situation. This is the case with the Time Traveller, with the Angel in *The Wonderful Visit* and with Prendick in *The Island of Dr Moreau*, while Griffin in *The Invisible Man* becomes the victim of his environment in attempting to control it. In all these novels, themes and motifs frequently recur so that cross-reference is inevitable when discussing them. Though Wells is a writer of symbolic fiction—or a myth-maker— the symbolism is not of the specifically 'heraldic' kind that we associate, for instance with Hawthorne's scarlet letter, Melville's white whale, or James's golden bowl. In Wells the symbolic element is inherent in the total fictional situation and to this extent he is closer to Kafka. When, for instance, we see in *The Time Machine* a paradisal world on the surface of the earth inhabited by beautiful carefree beings leading a wholly aesthetic existence, and a diabolic or demonic world beneath the surface inhabited by brutish creatures who spend most of their time in darkness in underground machine shops, and only appear on the surface at night, and when we are told that these two races are the descendants respectively of the present-day bourgeoisie and proletariat, and that the latter live by cannibalistically preying on the former—then clearly we are faced with a symbolic situation of considerable complexity, where several different 'mythical' interpretations are possible.

The hero of *The Time Machine*—unlike his predecessor, Nebogipfel, and his successors, Moreau and Griffin—is not a solitary eccentric on the Frankenstein model, but an amiable and gregarious bourgeois. Like Wells himself, he appears to be informed and interested in the dominant intellectual movements of his age, Marxism and Darwinism. Wells had come across Marx at South Kensington, and though in later years he was to become extremely anti-Marxist, it appears that in his immediate post-student days he was prepared to uphold Marxian socialism as 'a new thing based on Darwinism'.[41] However doubtfully historical this may be, the juxtaposition of the two names is very important for Wells's early imaginative and speculative writing. The time traveller, immediately after he has arrived in the world of 802701, is full of forebodings about the kind of humanity he may discover:

What might not have happened to men? What if cruelty had grown into a common passion? What if in this interval the race had lost its manliness, and had developed into something inhuman, unsympathetic, and overwhelmingly powerful? I might seem some old world savage animal, only the more dreadful and disgusting for our common likeness—a foul creature to be incontinently slain (4).

On a purely thematic level, *The Time Machine* can be considered as a development and expansion of the kind of speculation contained in 'The Man of the Year Million', though with a number of important differences. The Traveller, during his sojourn in 802701, is involved in a series of discoveries, both physical and intellectual. The more he finds out about the Eloi—and subsequently the Morlocks—and their way of life, the more radically he has to reformulate his previous theories about them. The truth, in each case, turns out to be more unpleasant than he had thought.

At first, however, his more fearful speculations are not fulfilled. Instead of 'something unhuman, unsympathetic and overwhelmingly powerful', he discovers the Eloi, who are small, frail and beautiful. He is rather shocked and then amused by their child-like ways and manifest lack of intellectual powers—'the memory of my confident anticipations of a profoundly grave and intellectual posterity came, with irresistible merriment, to my mind' (5). Such a 'grave and intellectual posterity' had in fact been postulated by Bulwer Lytton in *The Coming Race* (1871), a work which, it has been suggested, had some influence on *The Time Machine*, though the resemblances are very slight.[42] But it is quite possible that Wells was here alluding to Bulwer Lytton's romance, as well as to the wider implications of optimistic evolutionary theory.

Subsequently the Traveller becomes charmed with the Eloi and the relaxed communism of their way of life. They live, not in separate houses, but in large semi-ruinous buildings of considerable architectural splendour, sleeping and eating there communally. Their only food is fruit, which abounds in great richness and variety, and they are described in a way which suggests the figures of traditional pastoral poetry: 'They spent all their time in playing gently, in bathing in the river, in making love in a half-playful fashion, in eating fruit and sleeping' (8). The Traveller takes stock of their world:

I have already spoken of the great palaces dotted about among the variegated greenery, some in ruins and some still occupied. Here and there rose a white or silvery figure in the waste garden of the earth, here and there came the sharp vertical line of some cupola or obelisk. There were no hedges, no signs of proprietary rights, no evidence of agriculture; the whole earth had become a garden (6).

There appear to be no animals, wild or domestic, left in the world, and such forms of life as remain have clearly been subject to a radical process of selection:

The air was free from gnats, the earth from weeds or fungi; everywhere were fruits and sweet and delightful flowers; brilliant butterflies flew hither and thither. The ideal of preventive medicine was attained. Diseases had been stamped out. I saw no evidence of any contagious disease during all my stay. And I shall have to tell you later that even the processes of putrefaction and decay had been profoundly affected by these changes (6).

Man has, in short, at some period long since past obtained complete control of his environment, and has been able to manipulate the conditions of life to his absolute satisfaction. The 'struggle for existence' has been ended, and as a result of this manipulation, the nature of the species has undergone profound modification. Not only have the apparent physical differences between male and female disappeared, but their mental powers have declined as well as their physical. The human race, as it presents itself to the Traveller, is plainly in its final decadence. Wells had already dealt in 'The Man of the Year Million' with the possible ways in which the easing of environmental conditions would modify the species; but the men of the year million, as described in that essay, though physically much altered, had been both more intelligent and less beautiful than the Eloi (whose name carries several obvious associations, suggesting not only their *elfin* looks, but also *éloigné*, and their apparent status as an *élite*: there may also be a suggestion of *eld*, meaning old age and decrepitude). The Eloi, with their childlike and sexually ambiguous appearance, and their consumptive type of beauty, are clear reflections of *fin de siècle* visual taste.[43]

In the world that the Traveller surveys, aesthetic motives have evidently long been dominant as humanity has settled down to its decline. 'This has ever been the fate of energy in security; it takes to art and to eroticism, and then come languour and decay' (6). But in the age of the Eloi even artistic motives seem almost extinct. 'To adorn themselves with flowers, to dance, to sing in the sunlight; so much was left of the artistic spirit, and no more' (6). The first chapter of the Time Traveller's narrative is called 'In the Golden Age', and the following chapter 'The Sunset of Mankind'; there is an ironic effect, not only in the juxtaposition, but in the very reference to a 'golden age'. Such an age, the *Saturnia regna*, when men were imagined as living a simple, uncomplicated and happy existence, before in some way falling from grace, was always an object of literary nostalgia, and traditionally thought of as being at the very beginning of man's history. Wells, however, places it in the remotest future and associates it not with dawn but with sunset. The Time Traveller sees the Eloi as leading a paradisal existence, and his sense of this is imparted to the reader by the imagery of the first part of his narrative. They are thoroughly assimilated to their environment, where 'the whole earth had become a garden', and 'everywhere were fruits and sweet and delicious flowers: brilliant butterflies flew hither and thither'. Their appearance and mode of life makes a pointed contrast to the drab and earnest figure of the Traveller:

Several more brightly-clad people met me in the doorway, and so we entered, I, dressed in dingy nineteenth-century garments, looking grotesque enough, garlanded with flowers, and surrounded by an eddying mass of bright, soft-coloured robes and shining white limbs, in a melodious whirl of laughter and laughing speech (5).

The writing here suggests that Wells was getting a little out of his depth, but the intention is clearly to present the Eloi as in some sense heirs to Pre-Raphaelite convention. This implicit contrast between the aesthetic and utilitarian, the beautiful and idle set against the ugly and active, shows how *The Time Machine* embodies another profound late-Victorian preoccupation, recalling, for instance, the aesthetic anti-industrialism of Ruskin and Morris. The world of the Eloi is presented as not only a golden age, but as something of a lotos land, and it begins to exercise its spell on the Traveller. After his immediate panic on discovering the loss of his machine, he settles down to a philosophic resignation:

Suppose the worst? I said. Suppose the machine altogether lost —perhaps destroyed? It behoves me to be calm and patient, to learn the way of the people, to get a clear idea of the method of my loss, and the means of getting materials and tools; so that in the end, perhaps, I may make another. That would be my only hope, a poor hope, perhaps, but better than despair. And, after all, it was a beautiful and curious world (7).

The Traveller's potential attachment to the Eloi and their world is strengthened when he rescues the little female, Weena, from drowning and begins a prolonged flirtation with her. This relationship is the biggest flaw in the narrative, for it is totally unconvincing, and tends to embarrass the reader (Pritchett has referred to 'the faint squirms of idyllic petting').[44] But though the Traveller feels the attraction of the kind of life she represents, he is still too much a man of his own age, resourceful, curious and active, to succumb to it. As he says of himself, 'I am too Occidental for a long vigil. I could work at a problem for years, but to wait inactive for twenty-four hours—that is another matter' (7).

But it is not long before he becomes aware that the Eloi are not the only forms of animal life left in the world, and his curiosity is once more aroused. He realizes that Weena and the Eloi generally have a great fear of darkness: 'But she dreaded the dark, dreaded shadows, dreaded black things' (8). Here we have the first hint of the dominant imagery of the second half of the narrative, the darkness characteristic of the Morlocks, and the ugly shapeless forms associated with it, contrasting with the light and the brilliant colours of the Eloi and their world. Looking into the darkness one night just before dawn the Traveller imagines that he can see vague figures running across the landscape, but cannot be certain whether or not his eyes have deceived him. And a little later, when he is exploring one of the ruined palaces, he comes across a strange creature—'a queer little ape-like figure'—that runs away from him and disappears down one of the well-like shafts that are scattered across the country, and whose purpose and nature had puzzled the Traveller on his arrival: 'My impression of it is, of course, imperfect; but I know it was a dull white, and had strange large greyish-red eyes; also that there was flaxen hair on its head and down its back' (8). The Traveller now has to reformulate his ideas about the way the evolutionary development of man has proceeded: 'Man had not remained one species, but had differentiated into two distinct animals' (8). He has to modify his previous 'Darwinian' explanation by a 'Marxist' one: 'It seemed clear as daylight to me that the gradual widening of the merely temporary and social difference between the Capitalist and the Labourer was the key to the whole position' (8). Even in his own day, he reflects, men tend to spend more and more time underground: 'There is a tendency to utilize underground space for the less ornamental purposes of civilization' (8). 'Even now, does not an East-end worker live in such artificial conditions as practically to be cut off from the natural surface of the earth?' (8). Similarly, the rich have tended to preserve themselves more and more as an exclusive and self-contained group, with fewer and fewer social contacts with the workers, until society has stratified rigidly into a two-class system. 'So, in the end, above the ground you must have the Haves, pursuing pleasure and comfort and beauty, and below ground the Have-nots; the Workers getting continually adapted to the conditions of their labour' (8). The analysis represents, it will be seen, a romantic and pessimistic variant of orthodox Marxist thought; the implications of the class-war are accepted but the possibility of the successful proletarian revolution establishing a classless society is excluded. Thus, the Traveller concludes, the social tendencies of nineteenth century industrialism have become rigidified and then built in, as it were, to the evolutionary development of the race. Nevertheless, he is orthodox enough in his analysis to assume that the Eloi, despite their physical and mental decline, are still the masters and the Morlocks—as he finds the underground creatures are called —are their slaves. It is not long before he discovers that this, too, is a false conclusion.

Soon enough, despite his dalliance with Weena, and her obvious reluctance to let him go, the Traveller decides that he must find out more about the Morlocks, and resolves to descend into their underworld. It is at this point that, in Pritchett's phrase, 'the story alters its key, and the Time Traveller reveals the foundation of slime and horror on which the pretty life of his Arcadians is precariously and fearfully resting'.[45] The descent of the Traveller into the underworld has, in fact, an almost undisplaced mythical significance: it suggests a parody of the Harrowing of Hell, where it is not the souls of the just that are released but the demonic Morlocks, for it is they who dominate the subsequent narrative. During his 'descent into hell' the Traveller is seized by the Morlocks, but he keeps them at bay by striking matches, for they recoil from light in any form (which is why they do not normally appear on the surface of the earth by day). During his brief and confused visit to their world he sees and hears great machines at work, and notices a table spread for a meal. He observes that the Morlocks are carnivorous, but does not, for a time, make the obvious conclusion about the nature of the meat they are eating. However, it is readily apparent to the reader. The Morlocks have a complex symbolic function, for they not only represent an exaggerated fear of the nineteenth century proletariat, but also embody many of the traditional mythical images of a demonic world. This is apparent if one compares Wells's account of them and their environment with the chapter on 'Demonic Imagery' in Northrop Frye's *Anatomy of Criticism*. As Frye writes:

Images of perverted work belong here too: engines of torture, weapons of war, armour, and images of a dead mechanism which, because it does not humanize nature, is unnatural as well as inhuman. Corresponding to the temple or One Building of the apocalypse, we have the prison or dungeon, the sealed furnace of heat without light, like the City of Dis in Dante.[46]

Indeed, nothing is more remarkable about *The Time Machine* than the way in which its central narrative is polarized between opposed groups of imagery, the paradisal (or, in Frye's phrase, the apocalyptic) and the demonic, representing extreme forms of human desire and repulsion.

A further significance of the Morlocks can be seen in the fact that they are frequently referred to in terms of unpleasant animal life: thus they are described as, or compared with, 'apes', 'lemurs', 'worms', 'spiders', 'ants', and 'rats' (8, 9, 10, 12). One must compare these images with the Traveller's original discovery that all forms of non-human animal life—

with the apparent exception of butterflies—had been banished from the upper-world, whether noxious or not. There is a powerful irony in his subsequent discovery that the one remaining form of animal life, and the most noxious of all, is a branch of humanity. Furthermore, this confusion of human and animal—with its origin in an imaginative perturbation over the deeper implications of Darwinism—was to provide the central theme of *The Island of Dr Moreau*.

The traveller narrowly escapes with his life from the Morlocks, and returns to the surface, to make another reappraisal of the world of 802701. The image of the 'golden age' as it had presented itself to him on his arrival has been destroyed: 'there was an altogether new element in the sickening quality of the Morlocks—a something inhuman and malign' (10). He has to reject his subsequent hypothesis that the Eloi were the masters and the Morlocks their slaves. A new relationship has clearly evolved between the two races; the Eloi, who are in terror of dark and moonless nights, are in some way victims of the Morlocks, though he is still not certain precisely how. His experience underground has shattered his previous euphoria (symbolically, perhaps, an end of the paradisal innocence in which he has been participating), and his natural inventiveness and curiosity reassert themselves. He makes his way with Weena to a large green building that he has seen in the distance many miles off, which he later calls the 'Palace of Green Porcelain'. On their way they pass a night in the open: the Traveller looks at the stars in their now unfamiliar arrangements and reflects on his present isolation.

Looking at these stars suddenly dwarfed my own troubles and all the gravities of terrestrial life. I thought of their unfathomable distance, and the slow inevitable drift of their movements out of the unknown past into the unknown future. I thought of the great precessional cycle that the pole of the earth describes. Only

forty times had that silent revolution occurred during all the
years that I had traversed. And during these few revolutions all
the activity, all the traditions, the complex organizations, the
nations, languages, literatures, aspirations, even the mere memory
of Man as I knew him had been swept out of existence. Instead
were these frail creatures who had forgotten their high ancestry,
and the white Things of which I went in terror. Then I thought
of the Great Fear that was between the two species, and for the
first time, with a sudden shiver, came the clear knowledge of
what the meat I had seen might be. Yet it was too horrible! I
looked at little Weena sleeping beside me, her face white and star-
like under the stars, and forthwith dismissed the thought (10).

The Traveller's knowledge of the world of the Eloi and the
Morlocks, and the relation between them, is almost complete. When they reach the Palace of Green Porcelain, he
finds, as if to belie his reflections on the disappearance of all
traces of the past, a vast museum: 'Clearly we stood among
the ruins of some latter-day South Kensington' (11). The
museum, with its semi-ruinous remains of earlier phases of
human achievement, puts the Traveller once more in direct
emotional relation with the past, and, by implication, with
his own age. Here, the Arcadian spell is finally cast off. He
remembers that he is, after all, a late-Victorian scientist with
a keen interest in technology. He is intrigued by various
great machines, some half destroyed and others in quite
good condition:

You know I have a certain weakness for mechanism, and I was
inclined to linger among these: the more so as for the most part
they had the interest of puzzles, and I could make only the
vaguest guesses at what they were for. I fancied that if I could
solve their puzzles I should find myself in possession of powers
that might be of use against the Morlocks (11).

The Morlocks, after all, are a technological race, and if he is
to defend himself against them—as he has decided he must—

he must match himself against their mechanical prowess. The images of machinery in this part of the narrative are sufficient to suggest to the reader the presence of the Morlocks, and before long the Traveller sees footprints in the dust around him, and hears noises coming from one end of a long gallery, which means that the Morlocks are not far away. He breaks an iron lever off one of the machines to use as a mace. By now, his feelings for the Morlocks are those of passionate loathing: 'I longed very much to kill a Morlock or so. Very inhuman, you may think, to want to go killing one's own descendants! But it was impossible, somehow, to feel any humanity in the things' (11). Since the Morlocks on one level stand for the late nineteenth century proletariat, the Traveller's attitude towards them symbolizes a contemporary bourgeois fear of the working class, and it is not fanciful to impute something of this attitude to Wells himself. From his schooldays in Bromley he had disliked and feared the working class in a way wholly appropriate to the son of a small tradesman—as various Marxist critics have not been slow to remark.[47] The Traveller's gradual identification with the beautiful and aristocratic—if decadent——Eloi against the brutish Morlocks is indicative of Wells's own attitudes, or one aspect of them, and links up with a common theme in his realistic fiction: the hypergamous aspirations of a low-born hero towards genteel heroines: Jessica Milton in *The Wheels of Chance*, Helen Walsingham in *Kipps*, Beatrice Normandy in *Tono-Bungay*, and Christabel in *Mr Polly*.

Wells's imagination was easily given to producing images of mutilation and violence, and the Traveller's hatred of the Morlocks gives them free rein. The reader is further prepared for the scenes of violence and destruction which end the Traveller's expedition to the museum by his discovery of 'a long gallery of rusting stands of arms', where he 'hesitated between my crowbar and a hatchet or a sword' (11). But he could not carry both and kept the crowbar. He contented himself with a jar of camphor from another part of the museum, since this was inflammable and would make a useful weapon against the Morlocks. By now we have wholly moved from the dominantly paradisal imagery of the first half of the narrative to the demonic imagery of the second. Instead of a golden age, or lotos land, we are back in the familiar world of inventiveness and struggle.

When Weena and the Traveller are once more outside the museum and are making their way homeward through the woods, he decides to keep the lurking Morlocks at bay during the coming night by lighting a fire. He succeeds only too well and before long he has set the whole forest ablaze. Several Morlocks try to attack him, but he fights them off with his iron bar. He then discovers the creatures all fleeing in panic before the advancing fire: in the confusion Weena is lost. There are some powerful descriptions of the Morlocks' plight:

And now I was to see the most weird and horrible thing, I think, of all that I beheld in that future age. This whole space was as bright as day with the reflection of the fire. In the centre was a hillock, or tumulus, surmounted by a scorched hawthorn. Beyond this was another arm of the burning forest, with yellow tongues already writhing from it, completely encircling the space with a fence of fire. Upon the hillside were some thirty or forty Morlocks, dazzled by the light and heat, and blundering hither and thither against each other in their bewilderment. At first I did not realize their blindness, and struck furiously at them with my bar, in a frenzy of fear, as they approached me, killing one and crippling several more. But when I had watched the gestures of one of them groping under the hawthorn against the red sky, and heard their moans, I was assured of their absolute helplessness and misery in the glare, and I struck no more of them (12).

Eventually, on the following morning, the Traveller gets back to the neighbourhood of the White Sphinx, whence he had started. Everything is as it was when he left. The beautiful Eloi are still moving across the landscape in their gay robes, or bathing in the river. But now his disillusion with their Arcadian world and his realization of the true nature of their lives is complete.

I understood now what all the beauty of the overworld people covered. Very pleasant was their day, as pleasant as the day of the cattle in the field. Like the cattle, they knew of no enemies, and provided against no needs. And their end was the same (13).

Here we have the solution to a riddle that was implicitly posed at the beginning of the Traveller's narrative. Soon after his arrival among the Eloi he had found that there were no domestic animals in their world: 'horses, cattle, sheep, dogs, had followed the Ichthyosaurus into extinction' (5). Yet the life led by the Eloi is clearly that contained in conventional literary pastoral, and so the first part of the Traveller's narrative partakes of the nature of pastoral—but it is a pastoral world without sheep or cattle. And a little later, during his speculations on the possibilities of eugenic development, he had reflected:

We improve our favourite plants and animals—and how few they are—gradually by selective breeding; now a new and better peach, now a seedless grape, now a sweeter and larger flower, now a more convenient breed of cattle (6).

Something of this sort, he concludes, has brought about the world of 802701. But the paradox latent in the observation is only made manifest on his return from the museum, now possessing a complete knowledge of this world. There are no sheep or cattle in the pastoral world of the Eloi because they are themselves the cattle, fattened and fed by their underground masters. They are *both* a 'sweeter and larger flower' and a 'more convenient breed of cattle'. Thus, the complex symbolism of the central narrative of *The Time Machine* is ingeniously completed on this note of diabolic irony. Such knowledge has made the Arcadian world intolerable to the Traveller. He is now able to escape from it: the Morlocks have produced his machine and placed it as a trap for him, but he is able to elude them, and travels off into the still more remote future.

4

The final part of the Time Traveller's narrative, the chapter called 'The Further Vision', is an extended epilogue to the story of the Eloi and the Morlocks. The Traveller moves further and further into the future, until he reaches an age when all traces of humanity have vanished and the world is given over to giant crabs. The earth has ceased to rotate and has come to rest with one face always turned to the sun:

I stopped very gently and sat upon the Time Machine, looking round. The sky was no longer blue. North-eastward it was inky black, and out of the blackness shone brightly and steadily the pale white stars. Overhead it was a deep Indian red and starless, and south-eastward it grew brighter to a glowing scarlet where, cut by the horizon, lay the huge hull of the sun, red and motionless. The rocks about me were of a harsh reddish colour, and all the trace of life I could see at first was the intensely green vegetation that covered every projecting point on their south-eastern face. It was the same rich green that one sees on forest moss or on the lichen in caves: plants which like these grow in a perpetual twilight (14).

The whole of this vision of a dying world is conveyed with a poetic intensity which Wells was never to recapture. The transition from the social and biological interest of the '802701' episode to the cosmological note of these final pages is extremely well done: the previous account of the decline of humanity is echoed and amplified by the description of the gradual death of the whole physical world. The Traveller moves on and on, seeking to discover the ultimate mystery of the world's fate.

At last, more than thirty million years hence, the huge red-hot dome of the sun had come to obscure nearly a tenth part of the darkling heavens. Then I stopped once more, for the crawling multitude of crabs had disappeared, and the red beach, save for its livid green liverworts and lichens, seemed lifeless. And now it was flecked with white. A bitter cold assailed me. Rare white flakes ever and again came eddying down. To the north-eastward, the glare of snow lay under the starlight of the sable sky, and I could see an undulating crest of hillocks, pinkish-white. There were fringes of ice along the sea margin, with drifting masses further out; but the main expanse of that salt ocean, all bloody under the eternal sunset, was still unfrozen (14).

Finally, after an eclipse of the sun has reduced this desolate world to total darkness, the Traveller returns to his own time and the waiting circle of friends in his house at Richmond.

The *Daily Chronicle* in its enthusiastic review of the book, paid special tribute to these final pages, and referred to 'that last *fin de siècle*, when earth is moribund and man has ceased to be'.[48] This reference to the *fin de siècle* is appropriate both in its immediate context and in a larger sense; Max Nordau, in his attack on the *fin de siècle* mentality, had curiously anticipated the themes and dominant images of *The Time Machine*:

The old Northern faith contained the fearsome doctrine of the Dusk of the Gods. In our days there have arisen in more highly developed minds vague qualms of a Dusk of the Nations, in which all suns and all stars are gradually waning, and mankind with all its institutions and creations is perishing in the midst of a dying world.[49]

I have endeavoured to examine *The Time Machine* in terms of its structure and narrative development. Since it is a romance and not a piece of realistic fiction, it conveys its meaning in poetic fashion through images, not by the revelation of character in action. It is, in short, a myth, which in Shanks's words, 'can be interpreted in many ways, none of them quite consistent, all of them more alive and fruitful than the rigid allegorical correspondence'. I have indicated the various thematic strands to be found in the work. Some of them are peculiarly of their period, others have a more general and perhaps more fundamental human relevance. The opposition of Eloi and Morlocks can be interpreted in terms of the late nineteenth-century class-struggle, but it also reflects an opposition between aestheticism and utilitarianism, pastoralism and technology, contemplation and action, and ultimately, and least specifically, between beauty and ugliness, and light and darkness. The book not only embodies the tensions and dilemmas of its time, but others peculiar to Wells himself, which a few years later were to make him cease to be an artist and become a propagandist. Since the tensions are imaginatively but not intellectually resolved we find that a note of irony becomes increasingly more pronounced as the Traveller persists in his disconcerting exploration of the world in which he has found himself. *The Time Machine* is not only a myth, but an ironic myth, like many other considerable works of modern literature. And despite the complexity of its thematic elements, Wells's art is such that the story is a skilfully wrought imaginative whole, a single image.

CHAPTER III

THE SHORT STORIES

I

IN addition to *The Chronic Argonauts* Wells published a
number of shorter stories in the *Science Schools Journal*.
During the next few years, when most of his time was taken
up with tutoring, he appears to have abandoned writing
stories, together with most other forms of literary activity.
But early in 1894, when he had become a free-lance journal-
ist, he was contributing stories to *Truth* and the *St James's
Gazette*. The success of Kipling had helped to make the short
story something of a fashionable form; there was ample
room for such pieces in the sizeable weekly and daily papers
of the time, and there was beginning to be a distinct demand
for them, a demand which Wells was more than ready to
fill. In an uncollected newspaper article of 1893 Wells suggested that the books of the future will be shorter, 'a spray
of short stories instead of a Niagara of narrative, in which
respect Mr Rudyard Kipling is in advance of his age'.[1]
Certainly he learnt from Kipling, whose influence is apparent
in the opening pages of *The Time Machine*, while a story such
as 'The Flying Man' is openly derivative. As Wells relates in
his autobiography,[2] in the summer of 1894 he met Lewis
Hind, then editing the *Pall Mall Budget* (in which 'The Man
of the Year Million' had appeared the previous year), who
invited him to contribute a series of 'single sitting stories'.
These appeared at quite frequent intervals, and in 1895 most
of them were reprinted in Wells's first collection of short

stories, *The Stolen Bacillus and Other Incidents*, which was published by Methuen in November. The stories in this book are predictably uneven: some are merely expansions of facetious or sensational incidents, which bear obvious signs of their journalistic origin, but others possess, on a small scale, something of the imaginative distinction which had marked *The Time Machine*. As we have seen, *The Time Machine* itself, certainly Wells's finest literary achievement, originated in a similar commission by W. E. Henley to contribute a series of articles to the *National Observer*. Wells himself was to remark of some of these early stories, 'I would discover I was peering into remote and mysterious worlds ruled by an order logical indeed but other than our common sanity.' [a]

A representative story from *The Stolen Bacillus* is 'The Remarkable Case of Davidson's Eyes'. Here we find a recurring element in Wells's early imaginative writing, the apposition of contemporary reality with some wholly 'other' setting of a remote and exotic kind, a theme already made manifest in the encounter between the Time Traveller and the Eloi. Sidney Davidson, a rather ordinary young scientist, is conducting an experiment in a laboratory during a thunderstorm. As a result his vision becomes disordered in some mysterious way, so that whilst he continues to be physically present in North London he is living *visually* on an uninhabited island somewhere on the other side of the world. In his everyday surroundings he is quite helpless and has to be led about like a blind man. There is no specifically dramatic interest in this story, but Wells exploits to the full the weird potentialities inherent in the situation. When Davidson is taken downhill in London his vision similarly descends on the island, so that at certain points he sees and describes a strange undersea world of luminous fishes, though he can still hear people passing in the London street and a newsboy selling papers. Very gradually he begins to recover his normal vision; a 'hole' appears in his phantom world, and he sees part of his friend's hand: 'It looks like the ghost of a bit of your hand sticking out of the darkling sky.' As his normal vision returns the 'other' world becomes fainter and in time disappears altogether. Some years later Davidson recognizes from a photograph a ship he had noticed off the coast of the island, and he discovers from an officer who had been on the ship that the island really exists: a remote rock in the Antipodes inhabited only by penguins.

Up to this point Wells, or rather his sceptical and hard-headed narrator, Bellows, has only been concerned with the facts of the case and has made no attempt to give an explanation. So far, the story could be taken as a kind of ghost-story, or at least a pure mystery without any hint of a rational explanation. Bellows is more concerned with pre-senting the facts than with speculating about their possible cause, but in the final paragraphs he rather reluctantly puts forward the views of his scientific superior, Professor Wade:

That completes the remarkable story of Davidson's eyes. It's per-haps the best authenticated case in existence of real vision at a distance. Explanation there is none forthcoming, except what Prof. Wade has thrown out. But his explanation invokes the Fourth Dimension, and a dissertation on theoretical kinds of space. To talk of there being a 'kink' in space seems mere non-sense to me; it may be because I am no mathematician. When I said that nothing would alter the fact that the place is eight thousand miles away, he answered that two points might be a yard away on a sheet of paper, and yet be brought together by bending the paper round. The reader may grasp his argument, but I certainly do not. His idea seems to be that Davidson, stoop-ing between the poles of the big electro-magnet, had some extraordinary twist given to his retinal elements through the sudden change in the field of force due to the lightning. He thinks, as a consequence of this, that it may be possible to live visually in one part of the world, while one lives bodily in another. He has even made some experiments in support of his views; but, so far, he has simply succeeded in blinding a few dogs. I believe that is the net result of his work, though I have not seen him for some weeks. . . . But the whole of his theory seems fantastic to me. The facts concerning Davidson stand on an altogether different footing, and I can testify personally to the accuracy of every detail I have given.

Bellows, in his positivistic devotion to facts and his dislike of the 'fantastic', attempts to discourage us from accepting Professor Wade's explanation. Paradoxically, if, like Bellows, we do not accept it we shall be forced to move into the realms of mystery and the occult for an explanation, for the bare facts themselves are unlikely to satisfy us for long. Yet Bellows—as Wells uses him to manipulate the argument—invites us by his very obtuseness to accept Wade's explanation: 'The reader may grasp his argument, but I certainly do not.' Wells is here returning to the preoccupation of his student days with the Fourth Dimension and multidimensional geometries, which recurs in various forms in *The Chronic Argonauts* and *The Time Machine*, as well as in *The Wonderful Visit* and 'The Plattner Story'. It is a point of interest that the notion of a 'kink' in space has since become a commonplace to writers of science fiction. The explanation, so off-handedly presented by Bellows, seems unlikely enough, it is true, but at the same time, we are constrained to think that there might be something in it. It is in this area between the improbable and the impossible that Wells achieves many of his successes.

It is instructive to compare the technique that Wells here employs with that of one of his contemporaries, Arthur Machen, whose romances and occult tales were popular in the nineties. In places Machen attempts—quite unsuccessfully, I think—to combine scientific and occult elements, in contrast to Wells, who carefully separates and balances them. Here, for instance, is a passage from Machen's *novella, The Great God Pan*:

You may look in Browne Faber's book, if you like, and you will find that to the present day men of science are unable to account for the presence, or to specify the functions, of a certain group of nerve-cells in the brain. That group is, as it were, land to let, a mere waste place for fanciful theories. I am not in the position of Browne Faber and the specialists; I am perfectly instructed as to the possible functions of those nerve-centres in the scheme of things. With a touch I can bring them into play: with a touch, I say, I can set free the current, with a touch I can complete the communication between this world of sense and—we shall be able to finish the sentence later on. Yes, the knife is necessary; but think what that knife will effect. It will level utterly the solid wall of sense, and probably, for the first time since man was made, a spirit will gaze on a spirit-world. Clarke, Mary will see the god Pan![4]

At first glance, this may appear reminiscent of passages in Wells's romances, particularly the knowing reference to 'Browne Faber's book' and the casual mention of 'a certain group of nerve-cells in the brain' (though Wells would probably have made the latter phrase more specific). There is even something in the tone that suggests the explanations of their mysteries given by Moreau and Griffin. But Wells would never have been capable of the abrupt transition from brain-surgery to the spirit-world. Machen attempts here, and elsewhere in *The Great God Pan*, to give his occultism a scientific backing, but the attempt is not convincing. He was more at home in a world of strange Latin inscriptions and demonic possession than with the jargon of the laboratory or the surgery. In the passage I have just quoted the incantatory rhythms of the prose, and the repetitions of 'with a touch', suggest that Machen was trying to convince *himself* of the plausibility of what he was writing. One can contrast with this the casual assurance that Wells exhibits in the conclusion of 'The Remarkable Case of Davidson's Eyes', and in many other places in his fiction. And even when his writing was at its slackest, Wells would certainly have been incapable of the bathos with which Machen concludes this section of *The Great God Pan* (Dr Raymond has carried out the brain-operation on his ward, Mary, though with rather unhappy results):

'Yes,' said the doctor, still quite cool, 'it is a great pity; she is a hopeless idiot. However, it could not be helped; and, after all, she has seen the Great God Pan.' [5]

Machen's prose here suggests *The Young Visiters* rather than anything more terrifying.

Among the other stories in *The Stolen Bacillus* one that deserves special mention for its thematic significance is 'The Flowering of the Strange Orchid'. The central figure of this tale, which characteristically combines the light-hearted and the sinister, is Mr Winter-Wedderburn, a suburban gentleman who constantly complains of the emptiness of his life, and whose only passion is collecting orchids. At a sale he buys a new orchid of a completely unknown kind, which had been found in the Andaman Islands by a young collector who had died there. He plants the orchid in his hot-house and soon it starts putting out aerial rootlets that resemble tentacles and grow to a considerable length. One afternoon Mr Winter-Wedderburn does not come in for his tea; his housekeeper goes to the hot-house and finds him lying motionless on the floor:

The tentacle-like aerial rootlets no longer swayed freely in the air, but were crowded together, a tangle of grey ropes, and stretched tight with their ends closely applied to his chin and neck and hands.

With some difficulty he is extricated. He has lost a good deal of blood, but has sustained no further injury, and he soon recovers. On the immediately anecdotal level, the point of the story is that Mr Winter-Wedderburn has at last had the adventure for which he craves. Yet reading it in the context of Wells's other early novels and stories, one observes the recurring encounter between the exotic and the everyday. In 'Davidson's Eyes' the encounter was presented as a strange but passive superimposition of two worlds; here there is a violent collision: the quintessential bourgeois is the victim of the exotic flower that had already cost the life of a probably better man. It anticipates those later works which describe onslaughts made on contemporary bourgeois society by strange forces from outside its boundaries, or from outside the world itself: 'The Sea Raiders', 'The Star', 'The Empire of the Ants', and, above all, *The War of the Worlds*.

Another story from *The Stolen Bacillus* treats this theme rather differently, and in a much grimmer fashion. In 'The Lord of the Dynamos' Wells's capacity for myth-making is immediately apparent: this story has comparatively little of the careful realism that characterizes others in the collection, and its symbolic implications are more emphatic. In the opening paragraph we are presented with the two central figures: the electrician Holroyd, who runs 'the three dynamos that buzzed and rattled at Camberwell and kept the electric railway going', and his half-caste assistant, Azuma-zi. Holroyd is devoted to his machines and can be seen as a typical product of a technological society: 'He doubted the existence of the Deity but accepted Carnot's cycle, and he had read Shakespeare and found him weak in chemistry.' There is a sense in which Holroyd—presented in such terms —can be seen as faintly foreshadowing the admired scientific managers of Wells's later utopian fiction. But only faintly: in his other aspects Holroyd is something of a brute; he is a drinker and a bully, and makes a habit of systematically kicking Azuma-zi, whom he calls 'Pooh-bah'. In Holroyd Wells presents the paradigm of a strident and oppressive imperialism.

His victim and helper is described in the second paragraph, which begins, 'To define Azuma-zi was beyond ethnology.' Azuma-zi is an extraordinary mixture of African and Asiatic racial characteristics, and there is no doubt that he is to be seen as a generalized embodiment of the Non-European—of the 'other'—rather than a sharply realized personality. Holroyd and Azuma-zi are opposed on all points: the positivism of the one is contrasted with the superstitious proclivities of the other. Yet, if Azuma-zi comes to worship the large dynamo, it is because Holroyd has given him the idea:

Holroyd delivered a theological lecture on the text of his big machine soon after Azuma-zi came. He had to shout to be heard in the din. 'Look at that,' said Holroyd; 'where's your 'eathen idol to match 'im?' And Azuma-zi looked. For a moment Holroyd was inaudible, and then Azuma-zi heard: 'Kill a hundred men. Twelve per cent. on the ordinary shares,' said Holroyd, 'and that's something like a Gord!'

We have already been told that Holroyd 'doubted the existence of the Deity': we see here that his religious faculties have been focused, in a crude and secularized form, on to the dynamo. He worships the machine because of its vast and dangerous power—'Kill a hundred men'—and because of its importance to capitalist enterprise (of which Holroyd is a committed supporter; he is operating the dynamos as a blackleg during a strike)—'Twelve per cent. on the ordinary shares.' It is, indeed, 'something like a Gord', and as he dangerously remarks to the archetypal heathen, Azuma-zi, 'where's your 'eathen idol to match 'im?'

Azuma-zi becomes, in earnest, a worshipper of the great dynamo: 'His father before him had worshipped a meteoric stone; kindred blood, it may be, had splashed the broad wheels of Juggernaut.' His worship becomes steadily more overt and ritualistic, and the inevitable climax is reached with all Wells's narrative skill. One night there is a struggle, and Holroyd falls against the great dynamo where he is immediately electrocuted. His death is assumed to be an accident, and a substitute arrives. Azuma-zi prepares to give his god a second victim, but he is foiled in the attempt, and to evade capture he kills himself by grasping the naked terminals of the dynamo. The story concludes: 'So ended prematurely the worship of the Dynamo Deity, perhaps the most short-lived of all religions. Yet withal it could at least boast a Martyrdom and a Human Sacrifice.'

'The Lord of the Dynamos', despite its brevity, is a powerful piece of work, and its implications are complex. As its dominant imagery shows, it is, on one level, a kind of meditation on religion. The secularized Holroyd and the heathen Azuma-zi share a common god in the dynamo; but whereas Holroyd's is very literally a religion of 'service', Azuma-zi's is of an older and more full-blooded kind, which is accustomed to appease its god with human sacrifices. The clash of the two modes of worship proves equally disastrous for both adherents. In somewhat broader terms, the story can be seen as an image of the encounter between east and west, between—to put the distinction in perhaps excessively schematic language—the European consciousness that expresses itself in imperialism, technology and capitalism; and the Afro-Asiatic unconscious, that is drawn to the things of Europe but is still involved with dark gods and superstitions. Wells's language and symbolism are patently of their age; they recall Kipling, and perhaps the early Conrad (by anticipation, for Conrad had not yet published his first novel when 'The Lord of the Dynamos' originally appeared); but the situation that the story embodies and epitomizes is a central concern of the mid-twentieth century. In its purely mythical fashion 'The Lord of the Dynamos' is a more disturbingly prophetic work than many of Wells's later systematic attempts to plot the course of future events. Reading it, one is reminded of the Conrad of *Heart of Darkness* rather than the author of *Anticipations*.

2

The Stolen Bacillus was followed by three more collections of short stories: *The Plattner Story and Others* (1897), *Tales of Space and Time* (1899) and *Twelve Stories and a Dream* (1903). In 1911 Wells published *The Country of the Blind and Other Stories*, a selection from his four previous volumes together with some uncollected work. Many of the stories in these books are in Wells's realistic or comic vein, and do not fall within the scope of the present study.

The Plattner Story shows Wells expanding certain of the themes that he had outlined in his first collection. In the title story, the young schoolmaster, Gottfried Plattner, mysteriously disappears in an explosion during a chemistry lesson; when he reappears nine days later, it is discovered that his whole anatomical structure has been reversed: his heart is on the right, the position of his liver is similarly altered, and he is now left-handed. To account for this state of affairs, Wells reverts to his favourite motif of the Fourth Dimension:

To put the thing in technical language, the curious inversion of Plattner's right and left sides is proof that he has moved out of our space into what is called the Fourth Dimension, and that he has returned again to our world. Unless we choose to consider ourselves the victims of an elaborate and motiveless fabrication, we are almost bound to believe that this has occurred.

The facts of the case concerning Plattner are a graphic illustration of the mathematical truism that, just as a two-dimensional or 'flat' object can be turned over by lifting it into three-dimensional space, so the internal relationships of a three-dimensional body might be altered by removing it for the purpose into four-dimensional space. It is the kind of speculation that C. H. Hinton delighted to illustrate in his 'Scientific Romances' of the eighties.

However, this is no more than the intellectual basis for an ambitiously imaginative piece of work. Plattner's account of his time in the Other-World provides an elaborate example of the superimposition of the exotic and the mundane that Wells had previously sketched in 'Davidson's Eyes'. Its connection with the puzzle about the Fourth Dimension is, in fact, somewhat tenuous; Plattner's experiences in the Other-World exist on a different literary level from the bizarre transposition of his internal organs. It is true that in this story Wells pushes the contrast between the everyday world and its exotic opposite to an extreme: we have on the one hand the rather comic and pathetic young Plattner in his seedy private school—suggesting a first draft of Mr Lewisham—and on the other the dim green-lit world of the spirits who are constantly watching the living, with its suggestions of the *Inferno* and *Purgatorio* of Dante. It is arguable that this story is too ambitious in its structure to be really coherent: Wells is still separating and balancing the scientific and occult elements, but the balance is somewhat precarious. In terms of Wells's later fictional development 'The Plattner Story' has a special significance. In a few years he was to abandon romance for what he conceived of as his true vocation as a writer of realistic novels; in this story he was trying to combine the two elements within a single brief narrative.

I hope by now to have given an adequate account of the procedure of Wells's early stories. Among the other pieces in *The Plattner Story*, 'The Story of the Late Mr Elvesham' deserves mention as an essay in the purely occult: its substance might well have been used by Machen, but Wells's treatment is very different. 'The Red Room' is an attempt at a traditional ghost-story, though the presence in the reputedly haunted room is finally found to be not a malignant spirit, but fear itself.

In other stories the 'scientific' element popularly associated with Wells's romances is more pronounced. The apposition of the exotic and the mundane—or, more strictly, the scientific—is apparent in 'In the Abyss'. A diving-bell descends into the depths of the ocean and its occupant finds a city of reptilian bipeds, of quasi-human intelligence, who worship him as a visitant from heaven. One sees here, in a new guise, the theme of apotheosis that Wells had previously introduced in 'The Lord of the Dynamos'. 'The Argonauts of the Air' is a rather diffuse and extended piece, describing the first successful—though fatal—attempt of men to fly. It is noteworthy that when Wells wrote this story in 1895 he was inclined to regard the aeroplane as a somewhat remote and apocalyptic possibility: as late as 1901 he could only suggest that 'long before the year A.D. 2000, and very probably before 1950, a successful aeroplane will have soared and come home safe and sound'.[6]

I have already referred to 'The Sea Raiders' as being one of a group of stories that describe various attacks upon modern civilization. This account of the ravages of an unknown type of sea-creature upon the coasts of England and France is one of the most effective and economically told pieces in *The Plattner Story*; its sensational details are the more telling for being played down, and Wells makes a brilliant use of a semi-documentary style, with a wealth of irrelevant but persuasive details:

Until the extraordinary affair at Sidmouth, the peculiar species

Haploteuthis ferox was known to science only generically, on the strength of a half-digested tentacle obtained near the Azores, and a decaying body pecked by birds and nibbled by fish, found early in 1896 by Mr Jennings, near Land's End.

'The Sea Raiders' is an important example of what I have described as the 'fin du globe' myth, a central preoccupation of the final years of the nineteenth century. It was first adumbrated by Wells in his important essay, 'The Extinction of Man', which contains the germ of 'The Sea Raiders'; I shall give some account of this in Chapter V.

This preoccupation was expressed in specifically global terms in Wells's powerful short story, 'The Star', which was first published in 1897 and then collected in *Tales of Space and Time*. The theme of some cosmic catastrophe overwhelming the earth was by no means new (the story of the Flood can be taken as one of its archetypes), and Wells's treatment of it in 'The Star' may have owed something to Camille Flammarion's *fin de siècle* extravaganza, *La Fin du Monde*, published in 1894. Nevertheless, in the brilliance of its narrative technique and the controlled profusion of its images, Wells's story can be considered as entirely original. Here his prose reaches a level of poetic intensity that had only been surpassed in the vision of the dying world in the final pages of *The Time Machine* (the extent to which Wells's imagination could be fired by the theme of cosmic dissolution underlines his *fin de siècle* affiliations). The strange new planet wandering through outer space towards the solar system announces its presence to astronomers by irregularities in the motion of the planet Neptune; it becomes visible, and each night shines a little more brightly. Soon it becomes brighter than the moon, and finally hotter and brighter than the sun itself. In the earlier part of the story we are shown the effect of the star on human society throughout the world, in a series of vivid discontinuous images, but as the narrative approaches its climax and the star gets steadily nearer, we leave the world of men to contemplate the series of terrestrial disasters that the approach of the star brings about:

So the star, with the wan moon in its wake, marched across the Pacific, trailed the thunderstorms like the hem of a robe, and the growing tidal wave that toiled behind it, frothing and eager, poured over island and island and swept them clear of men. Until that wave came at last—in a blinding light and with the breath of a furnace, swift and terrible it came—a wall of water, fifty feet high, roaring hungrily, upon the long coasts of Asia, and swept inland across the plains of China.

Even when he is writing on this cosmic scale, Wells's sense of detail does not fail him:

The whole side of Cotopaxi slipped out in one vast convulsion, and a tumult of lava poured out so high and broad and swift and liquid that in one day it reached the sea.

And there is a similar effect when we are told that the snows of the Himalayas melted and poured down upon the plains of India. One might find fault with Wells's occasionally inflated use of language in 'The Star'—there can be no doubt that he regarded it as something of a set-piece—but this should not blind one to the brilliance with which he selects and juxtaposes his images of mounting catastrophe. His technique here is suggestive of the characteristic methods of post-symbolist poetry, as well as those of the cinema. The end of the story, when the destruction of the earth is narrowly averted, and mankind gradually recovers from its disasters, is inevitably somewhat anti-climactic: Wells's imagination lost its intensity when it was dealing with recovery rather than dissolution. The suggestion, in particular, that 'a new brotherhood grew among men' is out of keeping with what had gone before, and looks forward to Wells's later and very inferior novel, *In The Days of the Comet* (1906), which treats of a similar theme. 'The Star' may illustrate Nordau's complaint that for the *fin de siècle* mentality 'the prevalent feeling is that of imminent perdition and extinction'; it also shows what Wells was capable of when writing as a literary artist.

The theme of global dissolution is treated comically—and perhaps parodically—in another story in *Tales of Space and Time*, 'The Man Who Could Work Miracles'. The humble clerk, Fotheringay, discovers that he has the power to work miracles, and effects a number of modest changes in his environment, until, in order to give himself more time to complete his tasks, he unwisely requests the earth to stop rotating. Whereupon every object upon the surface of the earth flies off into space, Fotheringay included. For a paragraph or so Wells presents an image of universal destruction that recalls 'The Star'; then Fotheringay is able to collect himself sufficiently to wish that he could be restored—minus his miraculous gifts—to the point in time at which he found he possessed them. This is done, and the world is as it was before he commenced his miracle-working regime. This story—which is extremely entertaining—represents a new approach by Wells, since it combines seemingly occult elements with comedy or even sheer farce (already evident to some extent in *The Invisible Man*). The combination was to recur in several pieces in his next book. The other stories in *Tales of Space and Time* are 'The Crystal Egg', which provides another example of the now familiar juxtaposition of the exotic and the realistic; 'A Story of the Stone Age', an early example of the interest in the remote past that Wells was to express most fully in the early chapters of the *Outline of History*; and the *novella*, 'A Story of the Days to Come', which will be discussed in Chapter VI.

Those pieces in *Twelve Stories and a Dream* which might be classed as romances tend to show Wells's inventiveness rather than any profound power of imagination, though 'The New Accelerator' contains one of his most ingenious notions. Otherwise, they are less interesting rhetorically and conceptually than the stories in his previous volumes, and so reflect the parallel slackening of imaginative quality in his novels. Most of these stories were written for the *Strand*, a magazine which Wells found lucrative to work for (he told Arnold Bennett in 1901 that it paid him £125 for a story),[7] but which he also found artistically frustrating. In 1898 he had remarked in a letter to his father:

I'm also under a contract to do stories for the *Strand Magazine* but I don't like the job. It's like talking to fools, you can't let yourself go or they won't understand. If you send them anything a bit novel they are afraid their readers won't understand. Two stories they have had I consider bosh, but they liked them tremendously. Another I have recently done they don't like although it is an admirable story.[8]

3

The final efflorescence of Wells's talent as a short story writer is seen in two stories that he contributed to periodicals in 1904 and 1906; these are respectively 'The Country of the Blind' and 'The Door in the Wall'. In both of them the mythical note of his earliest work is once more evident; though they also contain elements which ultimately relate to Wells's personal preoccupations.

Superficially, as its title implies, 'The Country of the Blind' is a dramatization of the proverb, 'In the country of the blind, the one-eyed man is king'. The mountaineer Nunez stumbles by accident on a remote and inaccessible valley in the Andes, where all the inhabitants have been blind for centuries, and where the very concept of sight no longer exists. At first he arrogantly assumes that his possession of sight will enable him to become their master. However, he finds that the blind inhabitants' other faculties are so keenly developed that he is no match for them, and he has to make an act of abject submission. Finally they decide to remove his eyes, which they regard as anomalous growths on his face: at this he succeeds in escaping over the mountains, leaving behind the blind woman, Medina-saroté, with whom he had fallen in love. Yet the story is not concerned merely to refute one truism and substitute for it another, such as that pride goes before a fall, or that the seemingly weak may have more resources than the strong. It is more than a mere transmitter of proverbial wisdom. Some attention paid to the fairly obvious implications of its symbolism will reveal a much richer complex of meanings.

One must remark, initially, that of all Wells's essays in romance, 'The Country of the Blind' most closely approaches realistic fiction in its substance; there are no scientific elements here, and no obvious indulgence in fantasy at all. At the same time, in few of Wells's stories is the symbolism so suggestive. It must be admitted, by way of adverse criticism, that the prose is at times slack, and less precise and economical than in Wells's best work of the nineties, and the somewhat portentous manner of the first few pages is unfortunate. Nevertheless, the narrative movement is as vigorous and as well controlled as in any of the earlier works. Nunez is described to the reader as 'a mountaineer from the country near Quito, a man who had been down to the sea and had seen the world, a reader of books in an original way, an acute and enterprising man . . .' There is no question that Nunez is to be regarded favourably; he is a free, active and intelligent spirit; a two-eyed rather than a one-eyed man. Wells stresses early on, before Nunez completes his descent to the valley, that his sense of sight is keenly developed: 'among the rocks he noted—for he was an observant man—an unfamiliar fern . . . His first response to the windowless and parti-coloured houses of the blind inhabitants is visual and aesthetic: ' "The good man who did that," he thought, "must have been as blind as a bat." '

The village of the blind has been built in a way that accords functionally with their mode of existence, but to Nunez it presents a strangely urban and even bourgeois appearance, contrasting with the wildness of the mountains that surround the valley:

The irrigation streams ran together into a main channel down the centre of the valley, and this was enclosed on either side by a wall breast high. This gave a singularly urban quality to this secluded place, a quality that was greatly enhanced by the fact that a number of paths paved with black and white stones, and each with a curious little kerb at the side, ran hither and thither in an orderly manner.

The emphasis is on enclosure and regularity: the blind inhabitants have in fact made in this remote Andean valley a miniature approximation to the normal urban life of the civilized world. The valley-dwellers lead, in every sense, an enclosed life, and they cannot even conceive of a world existing outside their valley. Their degree of mental enclosure is apparent in their initial exchange with Nunez, who expresses himself in the spacious and visual terms appropriate to his nature:

'And you have come into the world?' asked Pedro.
'*Out* of the world. Over mountains and glaciers; right over above there, half-way to the sun. Out of the great big world that goes down, twelve days' journey to the sea.'
They scarcely seemed to heed him. 'Our fathers have told us men may be made by the forces of Nature,' said Correa. 'It is the warmth of things and moisture, and rottenness—rottenness.'

The blind people live in every respect in a closed world; it is even reflected in their cosmology:

They told him there were indeed no mountains at all, but that the end of the rocks where the llamas grazed was indeed the end of the world; thence sprang a cavernous roof of the universe, from which the dew and the avalanches fell; and when he maintained stoutly the world had neither end nor roof as they supposed, they said his thoughts were wicked.

The opposition between the blind and Nunez is absolute, for his visual delight in what they would deny is frequently stressed:

Nunez had an eye for all beautiful things, and it seemed to him that the glow upon the snowfields and glaciers that rose about the valley on every side was the most beautiful thing he had ever seen.

The implication becomes inescapable that Nunez's sight and his captors' blindness are to be read metaphorically as well as literally. Only very superficially is Nunez the would-be king of the country of the blind. He is, rather, the man who sees among those who do not see, the open mind among the conformists, a free spirit in a bourgeois world. Wells makes it clear that the blind are perfectly happy in their ordered, predictable mode of life; he seems to have been influenced in his conception by Johnson's picture of the Happy Valley in *Rasselas* (a book which he had first read as a boy): an enclosed world from which one ought not want to escape. Nunez's exploration of the world of the blind becomes successively more disturbing: structurally the story recalls the heuristic progresses made by the Time Traveller, the Angel in *The Wonderful Visit* and Prendick in *The Island of Dr Moreau*. The extreme development of the blind people's other senses means that his possession of sight gives him very little advantage, and in fact he is treated by them as an inferior being and systematically ridiculed and humiliated. He is unable to retaliate physically, for 'he discovered a new thing about himself, and that was that it was impossible for him to hit a blind man in cold blood'. The defeat of the would-be independent spirit by a conformist social order is a theme that meant a good deal to Wells, and it appears unmistakably in 'The Country of the Blind'. Wells's identification of social conformity with physical incapacity had been anticipated nearly ten years earlier in his novel, *The Wonderful Visit*, in which the Philosophical Tramp describes the villagers as 'pithed' (see below, page 93). The passing of time and the advent of totalitarian states which overtly aim at the crushing of individual consciousness has given a new dimension to 'The Country of the Blind'. It even hints at Orwell's *Nineteen Eighty-Four*. The scene in which Nunez is finally driven by hunger and sleeplessness and despair to conform to the accepted notions of the blind world is an alarmingly precise anticipation of the 'brainwashing' techniques of modern totalitarianism:

'I was mad,' he said. 'But I was only newly made.'

They said that was better.

He told them he was wiser now, and repented of all he had done.

Then he wept without intention, for he was very weak and ill now, and they took that as a favourable sign.

They asked him if he still thought he could '*see*'.

'No,' he answered. 'That was folly. The word means nothing—less than nothing!'

They asked him what was overhead.

'About ten times the height of a man there is a roof above the world—of rock—and very, very smooth.' ... He burst again into hysterical tears. 'Before you ask me any more, give me some food or I shall die.'

Yet 'The Country of the Blind' is more than a sociological or political fable. It reveals another aspect when we recall that Nunez reconciles himself to staying in the valley, because of his love for Medina-saroté: 'There came a time when Nunez thought that, could he win her, he would be resigned to live in the valley for all the rest of his days.' It is noteworthy that in this story Wells makes persistent use of certain archetypal images, and at this point we see Nunez, the man of light and air, an embodiment of the aspiring mind, who is constantly associated with the masculine imagery of high mountains, surrendering through love to a lifetime in a womb-shaped world, where the inhabitants live in perpetual darkness (and indeed sleep by day, and do their work by night). Here we see what Jung would describe as the surrender of *animus* to *anima*, of the masculine to the feminine principle. The ultimate surrender, both to social conformity and the dark forces of love, comes when Nunez reluctantly agrees to his masters' condition that he must be blinded—or, as they put it, that they must remove by surgery 'these irritant bodies', his eyes—before he can marry Medina-saroté. When he appeals to her by describing the visual delights of his world she is quite unable to understand him, and almost rebukes him: 'I know it's pretty—it's your imagination. I love it, but *now*——'

The themes of this story obviously have a wide human relevance, but at the same time they were extremely personal to Wells: one frequently finds in his other works the contention, implicitly or explicitly stated, that the demands of society and sexual love are both dangers to the free spirit of man. The idea that love is necessarily in conflict with masculine self-realization had been outlined in *Love and Mr Lewisham* (1900) and *The Sea Lady* (1902), and was to be fully developed in *The New Machiavelli* (1911) and *Marriage* (1912).

At the eleventh hour, just before he is to submit to his literal and metaphorical blinding, Nunez recovers his spirit, and turns his back on the valley, determined to escape to his own world. He sees the mountains, and 'It seemed to him that before this splendour he, and this blind world in the valley, and his love, and all, were no more than a pit of sin.' For a whole day he climbs the mountain barrier, and by nightfall he has surmounted it, though still very high up:

From where he rested the valley seemed as if it were in a pit and nearly a mile below. Already it was dim with haze and shadow, though the mountain summits around him were things of light and fire.

From having been a metaphorical 'pit of sin', the valley, far below him, has become a mere physical pit. Wells uses imagery brilliantly in the concluding sentences of the story. Nunez is once more in his own world, among physically beautiful things, ranging from the splendour of the mountain peaks to the delicacy of the lichen. But there is no certainty that he is able to descend again to the world of men; the implication of the final sentence, with its hint of menace in 'cold stars', is rather that Nunez perishes of exhaustion, content to have saved his soul by escaping from the Country of the Blind; death among the mountains is preferable to a living death among the blind.

The mountain summits around him were things of light and fire, and the little details of the rocks near at hand were drenched with subtle beauty—a vein of green mineral piercing the grey, the flash of crystal faces here and there, a minute, minutely beautiful orange lichen close beside his face. There were deep mysterious shadows in the gorge, blue deepening into purple, and purple into a luminous darkness, and overhead was the illimitable vastness of the sky. But he heeded these things no longer, but lay quite inactive there, smiling as if he were satisfied merely to have escaped from the valley of the Blind in which he had thought to be King.

The glow of the sunset passed, and the night came, and still he lay peacefully contented under the cold stars.

The end of the story expresses Wells's personal conviction that the individual can and should remove himself from any situation which he finds insupportable;[9] at the same time, it shows how the human spirit can assert its true freedom, even at the cost of physical extinction. 'The Country of the Blind' is a magnificent example of Wells's mythopoeic genius.

The last of Wells's short stories which I shall discuss is 'The Door in the Wall', which first appeared in the *Daily Chronicle* in 1906. In this story there is no exotic setting as in 'The Country of the Blind'; instead we are in the world of politics and affairs that Wells was to explore realistically a few years later in *The New Machiavelli*. The politician Lionel Wallace is, in the eyes of the world, a successful man; but, as he confides to the friend who tells the story, he has a 'preoccupation' that is gradually dominating his life and even affecting his efficiency. As a child of five he had wandered out of his home and through the streets of West Kensington, where he had noticed a green door set in a white wall. It was immensely attractive to him, and he had a very strong desire to open it and pass through (he somehow knew that it would be unfastened), but at the same time he felt an equally strong conviction that this would be wrong or unwise: in particular he felt his father would be very angry if he did so. Nevertheless, he yields to the temptation and finds himself in a beautiful garden. (One is reminded here of the garden which Alice sees through the little door in Chapter I of *Alice in Wonderland*.) Wells's account of the garden tries to give the sense of a child's paradise but is scarcely satisfactory; nevertheless, it can be accepted as shorthand for a type of *locus amoenus.* It has a rare and exhilarating atmosphere, its colours are clean and bright, and the child is filled with joy. There are rich flower-beds and shady trees, and various animals, including two splendid tame panthers. He meets a tall fair girl who 'came to meet me, smiling, and said "Well?" to me, and lifted me and kissed me, and put me down, and led me by the hand . . .' He meets other children and they play games together, though he cannot remember the games (a fact which later causes him much distress).

Then presently came a sombre dark woman, with a grave, pale face and dreamy eyes, a sombre woman, wearing a soft long robe of pale purple who carried a book, and beckoned and took me aside with her into a gallery above a hall—though my playmates were loth to have me go, and ceased their game and stood watching as I was carried away. 'Come back to us!' they cried. 'Come back to us soon!' I looked up at her face, but she heeded them not at all. Her face was very gentle and grave. She took me to a seat in the gallery, and I stood beside her, ready to look at her book as she opened it upon her knee. The pages fell open. She pointed, and I looked, marvelling, for in the living pages of that book I saw myself; it was a story about myself, and in it were all the things that had happened to me since ever I was born . . .

When the record of the book reaches the point at which he had found himself outside the green door, the whole enchanted world vanishes, and the little boy is once more in the dismal West Kensington street.

Throughout his later life he dreams of revisiting the garden, and at long intervals he has unexpected glimpses of the door in the wall, in different parts of London, but always when the exigencies of his immediate circumstances make it impossible—or at least, highly inconvenient—for him to stop and open the door. The child's vision, as Wells presents it, has all the marks of a return in fantasy to a prenatal state:

the door is an obvious womb-symbol. This suggestion is emphasized when we recall that Wallace's mother had died when he was two: the tall fair girl who greets him when he arrives in the garden, and the sombre dark woman who initiates him into the events of his life after birth (and who is referred to as 'the grave mother') can both be taken as aspects of the mother he had scarcely known. Yet Wells's picture is not exclusively Freudian in its implications; it also has elements of an older mode of regarding prenatal existence—the Wordsworthian. This is apparent in the reference to the children with whom the little boy plays, and who call him back when the dark lady draws him aside:

> Hence in a season of calm weather
>   Though inland far we be,
> Our Souls have sight of that immortal sea
>   Which brought us hither,
>   Can in a moment travel thither,
> And see the Children sport upon the shore . . .

After his mother died Wallace had been brought up by a governess; his father is described as 'a stern preoccupied lawyer, who gave him little attention and expected great things of him'. In the sphere of public life his father's expectations are fulfilled, for Wallace has an unusually successful career. Yet his constantly cherished secret desire to return to the garden represents a potential revolt against his father's authority; had he not, as a boy of five, felt that his father would be very angry if he went through the green door? We have here the elements of an Oedipus situation: ultimately Wallace destroys himself in daring to risk, for the second time, his father's displeasure, by opening the door and returning to the delectable world which he identified with his dead mother.

This fate is, in a sense, predictable, but on the narrative

86

level the way in which Wells brings it about is extremely adroit. Wallace tells his friend that three times in the past year he has seen the door, and on each occasion he has passed it by: once because he was on his way to a vital division in the House of Commons, once, significantly, because he was hurrying to his father's death-bed, and once because he wished, for reasons of personal ambition, to continue a discussion with a colleague. And now his soul 'is full of unappeasable regrets', and he is barely capable of working.

A few months later he is dead:

They found his body very early yesterday morning in a deep excavation near East Kensington Station. It is one of two shafts that have been made in connection with an extension of the railway southward. It is protected from the intrusion of the public by a hoarding upon the high road, in which a small doorway has been cut for the convenience of some of the workmen who live in that direction. The doorway was left unfastened through a misunderstanding between two gangers, and through it he made his way.

On the next apparition of the door, we may assume, Wallace resolved, at whatever cost, to open it and rediscover his garden; this represented a virtual and perhaps an actual abandonment of his career (and so struck, symbolically, at his father). At this point Wallace's visions—or hallucinations, if we prefer it—and the physical world around him were in fatal conjunction. There is a certain grim irony in the fact that the deep pit into which Wallace fell can be seen as just as much of a womb-symbol as the enclosed garden he was seeking. (The conclusion of 'The Door in the Wall' is, in a sense, antithetical to that of 'The Country of the Blind': Wallace dies in a pit; Nunez is at least able to escape from one.)

'The Door in the Wall' is not a systematic Freudian

parable, and it would be a mistake to try to treat it as one, just as it would be a mistake to over-emphasize the Jungian implications of 'The Country of the Blind'. With both stories I have merely tried to indicate ways of looking at their symbolism which seem to me illuminating. 'The Door in the Wall' has also a further and more personal dimension: the beautiful garden behind the closed door, with its rich and varied delights, can be readily taken as a symbol of the imagination, and Wallace as a projection of Wells's literary personality. At the start of his career as a writer he possessed a unique imagination, which flowered in a number of brilliantly original romances; yet after a few years he turned to realistic fiction, and then to works in which he tried to dragoon his imaginative powers for specifically didactic or even pamphleteering purposes; at which the quality of his original imagination deserted him. Here, perhaps, we see the implication of the closed door, glimpsed from time to time, but never opened again. Admittedly, 'The Door in the Wall' was published only in 1906, little more than ten years after Wells's early work appeared, but in such a volatile and changeable writer ten years of development is a long time. By then Wells was already becoming known as the author of *A Modern Utopia* and *Kipps* rather than of *The Time Machine*. The death of Wallace, in vainly trying to recapture his original vision, may relate to Wells's realization of the death of his original talent. 'The Door in the Wall' is one of Wells's finest stories; and it is almost the last he wrote.

CHAPTER IV

'THE WONDERFUL VISIT', 'THE ISLAND OF DR MOREAU', AND 'THE INVISIBLE MAN'

I

DURING the summer of 1895, in the months following the publication of *The Time Machine*, Wells was at work simultaneously on two more novel-length romances, *The Wonderful Visit* and *The Island of Dr Moreau*, and was soon to start writing a fourth, *The War of the Worlds*.

When *The Wonderful Visit* appeared in October 1895, the contemporary reception was, on the whole, favourable, though the precise nature of Wells's talent and artistic intentions was clearly puzzling to some readers. This fanciful account of the sudden descent of an angel into a quiet Sussex village was certainly in a very different vein from *The Time Machine*. In fact, it is wholly without any pretension to 'scientific' interest (if one excepts certain tentative speculations made by the Vicar about the Fourth Dimension). Like *The Sea Lady* of 1902, *The Wonderful Visit* is an exercise of pure fantasy which is much more likely to remind a modern reader of certain stories by E. M. Forster than of anything by Jules Verne. Both the *Review of Reviews* and the *Daily Chronicle*, in their notices of the book, compared Wells to F. Anstey,[1] though the latter remarked that Wells's satire proceeded 'upon a larger philosophic basis', and added, 'the irony of the book—the dramatic irony as opposed to the personal interpolations—is at times almost ferocious'. This was a perceptive comment, but in general *The Wonderful*

Visit does not seem to have prepared Wells's readers for the far more ferocious satire of *The Island of Dr Moreau* which was to outrage many critics the following year. Both works show, in varying degrees, the influence of Swift, whom Wells had been reading and whom he was always to admire.[2] But the ironical qualities of the book are to some extent masked by the sheer charm of the narration, which often approaches the merely whimsical but never succumbs to it. This quality was favourably remarked on by another contemporary reviewer, W. L. Courtney:

It would be indeed difficult to overpraise the grace, the delicacy, and the humour with which the author has accomplished his task . . . Rarely, amidst all the floods of conventional fiction-spinning and latter-day psychological analysis, does one come across such a pure jet of romantic fancy as that with which Mr Wells refreshes our spirits.[3]

A major element in the charm of *The Wonderful Visit* is the evocation of life in a small Sussex village on a few hot summer days in the mid-nineties. There is a similar evocation in *The Wheels of Chance*, published the following year, and in several more realistic novels, up to *Bealby* (1915). It is one of the central paradoxes of Wells that though he became increasingly a rebel and a utopian, inclined, like Nebogipfel, to think of himself as 'a man born out of his time', he was never wholly able to sever his emotional roots in the late Victorian Home Counties. The countryside of Kent, Sussex and Hampshire, usually imagined in conditions of perfect summer weather, forms a recurrent background to his fiction. Wells may be consciously satirizing the quasi-feudal village life of *The Wonderful Visit*, but he cannot conceal a certain affection for it.

As I have already suggested, there is a basic similarity between the narrative structures of Wells's first three romances. But in *The Wonderful Visit* he is not acting as myth-maker, as he had in *The Time Machine* and was to again in *Moreau*, but simply as a satirist, and the book's relation to the contemporary world is correspondingly more direct and less profound. In 1899 Wells remarked of it:

In 'The Wonderful Visit' I tried to suggest to people the little-ness, the narrow horizon, of their ordinary lives by bringing into sharp contrast with typical characters a being who is free from the ordinary human limitations.[4]

Wells here was attempting in retrospect to make *The Won-derful Visit* seem more specifically didactic than it actually was: the Angel was much less an ancestor of the Samurai of *A Modern Utopia* than these remarks might suggest. Never-theless, they can serve as an approximate statement of Wells's intention. He also observed that the original idea of the story was inspired by Ruskin's remark that if an angel were to arrive on earth the first thing men would do would be to shoot it.[5] In Wells's own writings, the germ of the novel can be found in an unsigned article, 'Angels, Plain and Coloured—a Neglected Branch of Science', that he contributed to the *Pall Mall Gazette* on 6 December 1893. Part of this article is reprinted in Chapter IX, 'Parenthesis on Angels', of *The Wonderful Visit*. There Wells writes:

Let us be plain. The Angel of this story is the Angel of Art, not the Angel that one must be irreverent to touch—neither the Angel of religious feeling nor the Angel of popular belief.

He is described as 'the Angel of Italian art, polychromatic and gay'. Apart from his wings, the Angel has a distinct resemblance to the Eloi of *The Time Machine*: like them, he is short and slender and very beautiful in a rather effeminate fashion, and wears a short coloured garment that leaves his legs bare (the latter detail scandalizes the Curate's wife and daughters, who imagine the Vicar is bringing home an insufficiently dressed young woman). This resemblance between Eloi and the Angel is not merely incidental, for it points to a specific link between the two works.

As we have seen, *The Time Machine* is polarized between images of beauty and ugliness, and the Angel takes over and continues the characteristic aestheticism of the Eloi, transposing it to the contemporary world. The Angel, in fact, is the medium for a critique of society that is fundamentally aesthetic in its mode of operation. 'The Land of Dreams' where the Angel has come from is not a human utopia, but a kind of aesthetic fairyland: 'It is Wonderland, with glittering seas hanging in the sky, across which strange fleets go sailing, none know whither. There the flowers glow in Heaven and the stars shine about one's feet and the breath of life is a delight' (7). This has the recognizable note of much minor *fin de siècle* writing. When the Angel makes his bewildered discoveries of contemporary life, first through the Vicar's explanations, and then by his own painful exploration, he is constantly finding that things are ugly or grotesque: the contrast already pointed early in *The Time Machine* between the Time Traveller, dressed in dingy nineteenth century garments, and the Eloi, is here expanded and given contemporary relevance. The beautiful Angel himself is made a grotesque figure by having to be dressed, for reasons of propriety, in clothes belonging to the Vicar.

Because it has an aesthetic rather than an ideological basis, the satire of *The Wonderful Visit* is of a general kind, attacking the absurdities inherent in the human condition itself, in the manner of Swift, or the late Wyndham Lewis, rather than some specific disorder in the social system. A critic such as Georges Connes, who sees *The Wonderful Visit* as indicative of Wells's socialist tendencies, has missed this point.[6] It is true that Wells emphasizes the contrast between the pleasant life of the Vicar and the hard life of the ploughman, toiling in the heat. Yet he also uses the 'Philosophical Tramp' whom the Angel encounters in Chapter XXX as a means of attacking the stupidity of the villagers, whom he says have all been 'pithed' (i.e. their brains have been removed and pith substituted, as vivisectionists treat frogs). When the Angel remarks on the ploughman, the tramp merely replies that he must certainly be 'pithed', 'else he'd be paddin' the hoof this pleasant weather—like me and the blessed Apostles'. Wells would have considered himself a socialist in the mid-nineties, but it is impossible to see any systematic sign of it in *The Wonderful Visit*.

The satire of *The Wonderful Visit*, though falling far short of Swift in its savagery, is wide-ranging enough to include the kind of faith in physical science with which the later Wells was to be identified. The pretensions of contemporary positivism are amusingly exposed in the person of the village physician, Dr Crump, a devoted reader of Nordau and Lombroso, who insists on regarding the Angel's wings as an anatomical deformity.

'Spinal curvature:' muttered Doctor Crump quite audibly, walking round behind the Angel. 'No! abnormal growth. Hullo! This is odd!' He clutched the left wing. 'Curious,' he said. 'Reduplication of the anterior limb—bifid coracoid. Possible, of course, but I've never seen it before.' The angel winced under his hands. 'Humerus. Radius and Ulna. All there. Congenital, of course. Humerus broken. Curious integumentary simulation of feathers. Dear me. Almost avian. Probably of considerable interest in comparative anatomy. I never did!—How did this gunshot happen, Mr Angel?'

A little later Crump, much to the Angel's alarm, suggests that he remove the 'abnormality' by surgical means.

If it wasn't for the bones I should say paint with iodine night and morning. Nothing like iodine. You could paint your face flat with it. But the osseous outgrowth, the bones, you know, complicate things. I could saw them off, of course. It's not a thing one should have done in a hurry——'

'Do you mean my wings?' said the Angel in alarm.

'Wings!' said the Doctor. 'Eigh? Call 'em wings! Yes—what else should I mean?'

'Saw them off!' said the Angel.

'Don't you think so? It's of course your affair. I am only advising——'

'Saw them off! What a funny creature you are!' said the Angel, beginning to laugh.

'As you will,' said the Doctor. He detested people who laughed. 'The things are curious,' he said, turning to the Vicar. 'If inconvenient'—to the Angel. 'I never heard of such complete reduplication before—at least among animals. In plants it's common enough. Were you the only one in your family?' He did not wait for a reply. 'Partial cases of the fission of limbs are not at all uncommon, of course, Vicar—six-fingered children, calves with six feet, and cats with double toes, you know. May I assist you?' he said, turning to the Angel who was struggling with the coat. 'But such a complete reduplication, and so avian, too! It would be much less remarkable if it was simply another pair of arms.'

The coat was got on and he and the Angel stared at one another.

'Really,' said the Doctor, 'one begins to understand how that beautiful myth of the angels arose . . .' (13).

A few pages later, Dr Crump talks to the Vicar in the absence of the Angel:

'That man,' said the Doctor in a low, earnest voice, 'is a mattoid.'

'A what:' said the Vicar.

'A mattoid. An abnormal man. Did you notice the effeminate delicacy of his face. His tendency to quite unmeaning laughter. His neglected hair: Then consider his singular dress . . .'

The Vicar's hand went up to his chin.

'Marks of mental weakness,' said the Doctor. 'Many of this type of degenerate show this same disposition to assume some vast mysterious credentials. One will call himself the Prince of Wales, another the Archangel Gabriel, another the Deity even. Ibsen thinks he is a Great Teacher, and Maeterlink a new Shakespeare. I've just been reading all about it in Nordau. No doubt his odd deformity gave him an idea . . .' (14).

The chapter in which the first of these entertaining passages occurs is headed, 'The Man of Science', and the irony informing it is of a significant kind to come from the young South Kensington graduate and former pupil of Huxley's. In fact, the young Wells was apt to be extremely sceptical of the possibilities of science, despite his training in it. This is apparent from the conclusion to his essay, 'The Rediscovery of the Unique', published in 1891:

Science is a match that man has just got alight. He thought he was in a room—in moments of devotion, a temple—and that his light would be reflected from and display walls inscribed with wonderful secrets and pillars carved with philosophical systems wrought into harmony. It is a curious sensation, now that the preliminary splutter is over and the flame burns up clear, to see his hands lit and just a glimpse of himself and the patch he stands on visible, and around him, in place of all that human comfort and beauty he anticipated—darkness still.[7]

Dr Crump is presented as a wholly farcical character, but he has significant affinities with Moreau, the central figure of Wells's next novel. Like Crump, Moreau thinks—and acts—exclusively in terms of surgery and anatomical manipulation.

Although the Angel is able to laugh at Crump's suggestion that his wings be removed surgically, he soon discovers that pain is one of the constant realities of the human condition. His awareness of the ugly and the grotesque soon merges

95

into an awareness of the inescapably painful. He enters on a process of unpleasant discoveries comparable to that made by the Time Traveller in the world of 802701. The malignancy of the Morlocks is recalled by that of the brutish village boys who pelt him with nuts, and at the very end of his short life in this world ugliness and pain are combined in his encounter with the barbed wire put up by Sir John Gotch, the local landowner. As in *The Time Machine*, the insufficiency of the aesthetic mode of being is demonstrated in violent terms. The Angel discusses the prevalence of pain with the Vicar:

'The strange thing,' said the Angel, 'is the readiness of you Human Beings—the zest, with which you inflict pain. Those boys pelting me this morning——'
'Seemed to enjoy it,' said the Vicar. 'I know.'
'Yet they don't like pain,' said the Angel.
'No,' said the Vicar; '*they* don't like it.'

.   .   .   .

'Then the animals. A dog today behaved most disagreeably. And these boys, and the way in which people speak. Everyone seems anxious—willing at any rate—to give this Pain. Everyone seems busy giving pain——'
'Or avoiding it,' said the Vicar, pushing his dinner away before him. 'Yes—of course. It's fighting everywhere. The whole living world is a battle-field—the whole world. We are driven by Pain. Here. How it lies on the surface! This Angel sees it in a day!' (33).

Here we are once more reminded that *The Wonderful Visit* was to be followed by *The Island of Dr Moreau*, where the possibilities of pain are explored with nightmarish intensity.

Though *The Wonderful Visit* was no doubt intended to be a wide-ranging satire on the human condition, and in places succeeds as such, the satire lacks intensity, and one is apt to remember the book rather for its generalized charm and humour. It has never had the reputation of the more 'scientific' romances that immediately preceded and followed it, and it lacks the symbolic or mythical qualities of *The Time Machine* or *The Island of Dr Moreau*. Nevertheless, it provides significant thematic links between these two works, and illustrates certain of Wells's fundamental attitudes.

2

Wells had expected *The Island of Dr Moreau* to be published in January 1896, three months after *The Wonderful Visit*, but in fact it did not appear until April of that year. In a letter to his brother, dated 24 January 1896, he blamed the delay on the crisis that had followed the Jameson Raid.[8] The critical reception of the book was far less favourable than that given to Wells's previous books. Some reviewers were so horrified by what they considered the blatant sensationalism of the novel that they were quite unable to consider its literary merits. *The Times*, for instance, considered that 'This novel is the strongest example we have met of the perverse quest after anything in any shape that is freshly sensational.' [9] The *Athenaeum* devoted two-thirds of a column to horrified denunciation of *Moreau*, though without giving any idea of the subject or theme of the story: 'The horrors described by Mr Wells in his latest book very pertinently raises the question how far it is legitimate to create feelings of disgust in a work of art.' [10]

There was a tendency to attack the book as though it were sexually offensive, even though this was not the case: 'In the present instance he has achieved originality at the expense of decency (we do not use the word in its sexual significance) and common sense . . .' [11] And Wells's colleague on the reviewing staff of the *Saturday Review*, Peter

Chalmers Mitchell, who was himself a trained biologist, wrote a long notice of the novel headed 'Mr Wells's "Dr Moreau"', which opened by admitting Wells's gifts—'We have all been saying that here is an author with the emotions of an artist and the intellectual imagination of a scientific investigator'—but went on to attack *Moreau*, more in sorrow than in anger, both for its failure in taste and sensibility, and for its propagating of various scientific impossibilities.[12] In particular, Mitchell argued that grafting operations could not be carried out on the scale shown in the book. After a delay of several months Wells replied to this particular criticism in a letter to the *Saturday Review* by referring to a recent article on grafting published in the *British Medical Journal*.[13]

Wells was irritated and perhaps surprised by these criticisms. In a magazine interview printed the following year he is reported as saying:

I should say that *The Island of Dr Moreau*, although it was written in a great hurry and is marred by many faults, is the best work I have done. It has been stupidly dealt with—as a mere shocker— by people who ought to have known better. The *Guardian* critic seemed to be the only one who read it aright, and who therefore succeeded in giving a really intelligent notice of it.[14]

The review in the *Guardian* to which Wells referred was certainly more balanced than some of the others, though the writer was still uncertain about Wells's intentions:

Sometimes one is inclined to think the intention of the author has been to satirize and rebuke the presumption of science; at other times his object seems to be to parody the work of the Creator of the human race, and cast contempt upon the dealings of God with His creatures. This is the suggestion of the exceedingly clever and realistic scenes in which the humanized beasts recite the Law their human maker has given them, and show very plainly how impossible it is to them to keep that law.[15]

This is a reasonably just account of the work, and in point of fact both alternative explanations are applicable. Wells implicitly acknowledged the truth of the latter interpretation when in 1924 he referred to *Moreau* as a 'theological grotesque'.[16]

Not all reviewers were shocked by the book, even though they may have had reservations of a literary kind. Richard Le Gallienne remarked, 'Some have shuddered, and called the book "revolting". Perhaps it is; but a still more serious objection to it, from my point of view, is that it fails to convince', [17] while Grant Richards wrote, 'Only here and there do the means by which horror is attained transcend the legitimate. The truth is, Mr Wells has an unusually vivid imagination, which sometimes runs away with him.' [18] But read over sixty years after its publication, *The Island of Dr Moreau* can still affect the nerves in an unpleasantly direct fashion, which is in itself evidence of its power. Whatever his stated intentions may have been, one cannot acquit Wells of a certain desire to *épater le bourgeois*, which proved in the event to be eminently successful. In fact the horrified reaction of many readers can be seen as not merely a response to passages of bad taste in the book, but, more significantly, as an unconscious recognition of the implications of its symbolism.

Whereas Wells's other novel-length romances draw to some extent on his own experiences for their setting and background (this is true even of *The Time Machine*, where the world of the Eloi is superimposed on the still faintly familiar topography of the Thames valley), *The Island of Dr Moreau* does not, for at the time he wrote it he had never been out of England, still less made a voyage to a remote

Pacific island. It is composed of extremely literary materials, and is, in fact, an example of what a Swiss critic, Richard Gerber, has recently described as 'the English Island' myth:

Even for the continental imagination, the concept of the island beyond the sea has always had a positive mythical aspect: Atlantis, Ultima Thule, Elysium. While such island myths are probably not more frequent in English than in continental poetry—and even if this were so they have not succeeded in affecting the continental imagination—in prose fiction English writers, being nearer island reality, have been able, as no others have done, to stamp the island myth indelibly on the continental mind: in *Robinson Crusoe*, in *Gulliver's Travels*, in *Utopia*. They are all of them 'world-books' and living myths for almost everybody. Of what other prose fiction in English literature can we safely say the same? And what other literature has produced anything similar, not only in the mere concept, but in general imaginative force and validity?[19]

The tradition was continued in the nineteenth century by certain immensely popular and influential boys' books, such as *Coral Island* and *Treasure Island*. An accomplished recent example is William Golding's *Lord of the Flies*. It is in this tradition that *The Island of Dr Moreau* takes its place; it may even be a demonic parody of another and older island story, *The Tempest*, for Moreau as king of the island, seems to be a perverted image of Prospero, while his drunken assistant, Montgomery, stands for Ariel, and the humanized bear, M'ling, for Caliban. But if Wells's novel takes its place in a long and venerable line of 'island myths', the myth, in this particular instance, is given vitality by the meaning which it conveys. And the meaning of the novel is to be found, I think, in one of the profoundest intellectual preoccupations of the second half of the nineteenth century: the implications of Darwinism.

For the popular mind, at least, Evolution had substituted

blind Chance, as a force governing the universe, for the beneficent attentions of a Deity. And Chance makes an appearance in the very first chapter of *The Island of Dr Moreau*: Edward Prendick, shipwrecked whilst crossing the Pacific, is drifting in a dinghy with two other men; after eight days they are almost dying for want of food and water. One of the two men proposes that they draw lots to determine which of the three will be killed and eaten by the other two (Wells's source for this incident may have been Poe's *Narrative of Arthur Gordon Pym*); for a long time Prendick resists this proposal, but he finally assents to it. Lots are drawn, and the victim is one of the other two men, who violently resists; there is a struggle and both men fall overboard, leaving Prendick alone in the dinghy. The incident has nothing to do with the narrative that is to follow, but it sets the emotional tone of the whole work, by demonstrating the savagery of nature, even—or especially— human nature, and by showing that survival can depend on pure chance.

Later, the dying Prendick is picked up by a ship, and he is restored by the dissolute young doctor Montgomery: significantly, he remembers being given a drink 'which tasted like blood, and made me feel stronger'. When he has recovered he tries to thank Montgomery:

'If I may say it,' said I, after a time, 'you have saved my life.'
'Chance,' he answered; 'just chance.'
'I prefer to make my thanks to the accessible agent.'
'Thank no one. You had the need, and I the knowledge, and I injected and fed you much as I might have collected a specimen. I was bored and wanted something to do. If I'd been jaded that day, or hadn't liked your face, well—; it's a curious question where you would have been now' (4).

The theme of chance is now made explicit; it is to reappear at the core of the book, in Moreau's explanation of his acts. As the ship approaches the nameless island to which Montgomery is conducting a cargo of animals, the drunken captain becomes extremely hostile to Prendick, and refuses to take him any further: ' "Overboard," said the captain. "This ship ain't for beasts and cannibals, and worse than beasts, any more." ' But Moreau, who is supervising the unloading of the menagerie, refuses to take him, so Prendick is once more cast adrift in the dinghy: the chapter in which this takes place is headed 'The Man who had Nowhere to go'. He is thrust out of the world of men, symbolized, however crudely, by the captain, but has not yet been accepted into Moreau's private world. Eventually, however, Moreau's launch picks him up and he is allowed to land.

For the next few chapters we follow Prendick in his exploration of the island and its inhabitants: the book corresponds to the now familiar heuristic pattern. We learn that, like Wells himself, he 'had spent some years at the Royal College of Science, and had done some research in biology under Huxley' (6). In the encounter between Prendick and Moreau we see the contrast between orthodox science and its alchemical counterpart: between Huxley and Frankenstein, to put it briefly. Moreau says that he and Montgomery are also biologists, engaged in research, and a little later Prendick remembers that Moreau had once been known in England as a distinguished physiologist, but some ten years ago had left the country after a scandal in which it was alleged he engaged in needlessly cruel processes of vivisection. The insistent cries of pain coming from a puma in Moreau's enclosure suggest that he has continued in these practices: the motif of pain, first introduced in *The Wonderful Visit*, is another dominant element in *The Island of Dr Moreau*. Prendick soon discovers that there is something extremely sinister about the island: the inhabitants are all ugly and misshapen, and despite their superficially human appearance and demeanour there is something about them inescapably suggestive of the animal world. Wells's account of Prendick's encounter with these creatures in Chapter XII ('The Sayers of the Law') seems to owe a good deal to the humanized beasts of Kipling's *Jungle Book* (1894), while the Law they chant, which they have been taught by Moreau, is almost a parody of 'The Law of the Jungle' in the *Second Jungle Book* (1895):

> Not to go on all-Fours; *that* is the Law.
> Are we not Men?
> Not to suck up Drink; *that* is the Law.
> Are we not Men?
> Not to eat Flesh nor Fish; *that* is the Law.
> Are we not Men?
> Not to claw Bark of Trees; *that* is the Law.
> Are we not Men?
> Not to chase other Men; *that* is the Law.
> Are we not Men?

Yet if the immediate literary influence is Kipling, the spirit here is closer to Swift, whose influence on the book Wells freely acknowledged.[20]

For the brutish islanders, it appears, Moreau is God; they go on to chant:

> *His* is the House of Pain.
> *His* is the Hand that makes.
> *His* is the Hand that wounds.
> *His* is the Hand that heals.

Prendick, who has had a horrifying glimpse of a surgical operation going on in the enclosure, is already convinced that Moreau and Montgomery are engaged in transforming men into animals, and that they have the same fate in store for him:

These sickening scoundrels had merely intended to keep me

back, to fool me with their display of confidence, and presently to fall upon me with a fate more horrible than death, with torture, and after torture the most hideous degradation it was possible to conceive—to send me off, a lost soul, a beast, to the rest of their Comus rout (11).

After he hears the creatures reciting the Law, 'a horrible fancy came into my head that Moreau, after animalizing these men, had infected their dwarfed brains with a kind of deification of himself'. Prendick assumes that Moreau is a modern version of Circe or Comus; despite his scientific training and outlook he instinctively assesses the situation in terms of a traditional myth. He is wrong in this, as we shall see, but he is right in imputing a self-assumed God-like role to Moreau. He eludes Moreau and Montgomery who are seeking him after he has disappeared from his dwelling; Prendick imagines they are hunting him, and he walks into the sea, prepared to drown or be eaten by sharks rather than undergo the tortures he imagines Moreau is waiting to inflict on him. Moreau, standing on the beach, tries to persuade Prendick that the creatures he has seen are not men transformed into animals, but rather animals who have been partially humanized. Finally, Prendick agrees to return and listen to Moreau's explanation.

This explanation, which occurs in Chapter XIV—'Dr Moreau Explains'—forms the core of the book, and was originally published by Wells as a separate essay under the title 'The Limits of Individual Plasticity'.[21] Here Moreau describes how he employs his great knowledge of anatomy and surgical skill to remould various kinds of animal life into an approximate likeness of humanity. He appears not only as Prospero, manipulating the normal processes of nature to his own pleasure, but as God: not the traditional God of Christian theology, but the sort of arbitrary and impersonal power that might be conceived of as lying behind the evolutionary process. One recalls an earlier Victorian imaginative response to Evolution, Browning's 'Caliban upon Setebos', where Caliban muses upon the total arbitrariness of his god, Setebos:

> Put case, unable to be what I wish,
> I yet would make a live bird out of clay:
> Would not I take clay, pinch my Caliban
> Able to fly?—for, there, see, he hath wings,
> And great comb like the hoopoe's to admire,
> And there, a sting to do his foes offence,
> There, and I will that he begin to live,
> Fly to yon rock-top, nip me off the horns
> Of grigs high up that make the merry din,
> Saucy through their veined wings, and mind me not.
> In which feat, if his leg snapped, brittle clay,
> And he lay stupid-like,—why, I should laugh;
> And if he, spying me, should fall to weep,
> Beseech me to be good, repair his wrong,
> Bid his poor leg smart less or grow again,—
> Well, as the chance were, this might take or else
> Not take my fancy; I might hear his cry,
> And give the manikin three sound legs for one,
> Or pluck the other off, leave him like an egg,
> And lessoned he was mine and merely clay.

We have already encountered similar sentiments in *The Island of Dr Moreau*, from Montgomery, when Prendick had thanked him for saving his life. And with Moreau's explanation the dominance of chance in his universe is emphasized:

But I asked him why he had taken the human form as a model. There seemed to me then, and there still seems to me now, a strange wickedness in that choice.

He confessed that he had chosen that form by chance. 'I might just as well have worked to form sheep into llamas, and llamas into sheep. I suppose there is something in the human form that appeals to the artistic turn of mind more powerfully than any animal shape can. But I've not confined myself to man-making. Once or twice . . .' (4).

(One is reminded of Wells in a very different vein: the hero of his humorous short story, 'The Triumphs of a Taxidermist', says, 'I have *created* birds . . . *New* birds. Improvements. Like no birds that was ever seen before.')

Moreau is not only a nightmarish caricature of the Almighty: he can also be seen as a hypostatized image of the pretensions of science, already foreshadowed by the surgically-minded Dr Crump in *The Wonderful Visit*, despite the great differences in tone and treatment between the books. Yet he also is contrasted with the orthodox and humane scientist, Prendick, the former pupil of Huxley. Moreau is both a traditional and a contemporary figure, and his most obvious literary progenitors are Mary Shelley's Frankenstein and Stevenson's Jekyll-Hyde. (In 1914 Thomas Seccombe remarked of *The Island of Dr Moreau*, '*Membra disjecta* from "Gulliver's Fourth Voyage", "Jekyll and Hyde" and "Frankenstein", could perhaps be detected in it.')[22] Prendick's association with Huxley is not, I think, purely arbitrary: three years before *The Island of Dr Moreau* appeared, Huxley had delivered at Oxford his Romanes lecture, *Evolution and Ethics*, a powerful summary of the moral dilemmas with which the theory and practice of Evolution confronted the late-Victorian world. For Huxley, Nature, as manifested in evolutionary processes, was cruel and arbitrary, and ethical progress could only be made in opposition to it: 'Let us understand, once for all, that the ethical progress of society depends, not on imitating the cosmic process, still less in running away from it, but in combating it.'[23] Huxley and Moreau would agree about the characteristics of natural processes, but would differ diametrically about the attitudes to be adopted towards them: for Huxley, they must be opposed in the interests of ethics; for Moreau, who is untroubled by ethical considerations, they should be imitated in the pursuit of pure knowledge:

'To this day I have never troubled about the ethics of the matter. The study of Nature makes a man at last as remorseless as Nature. I have gone on, not heeding anything but the question I was pursuing, and the material has . . . dripped into the huts yonder . . .' (14).

Perversely, Moreau seems to adopt certain of Huxley's notions to his own ends. Huxley had argued that 'suffering is the badge of all sentient beings'; Moreau implies that pain could be a specifically humanizing agency (an opinion of which Peter Chalmers Mitchell was specially critical):

Each time I dip a living creature into the bath of burning pain, I say, this time I will burn out all the animal, this time I will make a rational creature of my own. After all, what is ten years? Man has been a hundred thousand in the making (14).

He considers that man should be superior to pain or pleasure:

This store men and women set on pleasure and pain, Prendick, is the mark of the beast upon them, the mark of the beast from which they came. Pain! Pain and pleasure—they are for us only so long as we wriggle in the dust . . . (14)

As I have already suggested, Moreau's superiority to conventional ethics, and his desire to make a new man on his own terms, seem to reflect the influence of Nietzsche, though the chapter was written before Nietzsche's work was generally known in England. Certainly Moreau can stand as a symbol of the Nietzschean 'transvaluation of values'. The theatrical aspects of Wells's presentation of Moreau should not blind us to the alarming implications of what he symbolizes: he stands for both science—unhindered by the ethical considerations which had concerned Huxley—and evolutionary nature, in all its violence and arbitrariness: 'The study of Nature makes a man at last as remorseless as Nature.' He is Frankenstein—the would-be creator of life—in a post-Darwinian guise.

In the days following Moreau's explanation, Prendick takes stock of his surroundings and even becomes a little habituated to them. He learns that Moreau has conditioned the Beast People to repeat the Law, and they try to abide by it, though it is in conflict with the promptings of their still animal natures; but for all their repetitions, they frequently break it. Without being specifically derivative, the tone of the novel becomes increasingly reminiscent of the Fourth Book of *Gulliver's Travels*:

I would see one of the clumsy bovine creatures who worked the launch treading heavily through the undergrowth, and find myself asking, trying hard to recall, how he differed from some really human yokel trudging home from his mechanical labours . . . (15).

Prendick is already sufficiently under the spell of Moreau's world to see resemblances between humanity and Moreau's imitations of it. But Moreau's authority over the island and its creatures is not to remain undisputed for much longer. As if the intrusion of Prendick from the outside world represented a disrupting influence, the precarious equilibrium that Moreau has established begins to break up, and the latter half of the novel is a record of ever-increasing physical and moral disintegration. The Swiftian note becomes more pronounced, and the symbolic elements are stressed almost to the point of allegory:

A strange persuasion came upon me that, save for the grossness of the line, the grotesqueness of the forms, I had here before me

the whole balance of human life in miniature, the whole inter-
play of instinct, reason, and fate, in its simplest form . . . (16).

I must confess I lost faith in the sanity of the world when I saw
it suffering the painful disorder of this island. A blind fate, a vast
pitiless mechanism, seemed to cut and shape the fabric of existence, and I, Moreau (by his passion for research), Montgomery
(by his passion for drink), the Beast People, with their instincts
and mental restrictions, were torn and crushed, ruthlessly, inevitably, amid the infinite complexity of its incessant wheels
(16).

The anticipated catastrophe is not long in coming. One
day the tormented puma breaks loose and kills Moreau (just
as Frankenstein's death was brought about by the monster
he had created). Now that their god is dead, the humanized
beasts abandon their allegiance to the Law and commence
their slow but inevitable reversion to the animal condition;
the process is paralleled in Montgomery, who gives himself up wholly to drink, and even, disastrously, gives brandy
to some of the Beast People. As Prendick says, 'You've made
a beast of yourself. To the beasts you may go.' Soon these
drunken creatures turn on Montgomery and kill him; his
dying words are: 'the last of this silly universe. What a
mess——'

Prendick is now completely alone: the dwellings and enclosure have accidentally caught fire and been consumed (a
detail forgotten by V. S. Pritchett, who has remarked that
there are fires in all Wells's early romances, *except The
Island of Dr Moreau*); he also finds that Montgomery, in a fit
of drunken spite, has burnt the two boats, so there is no
means of escaping from the island. The process of alienation
that began when Prendick was thrust out of the world of
normal humanity by the captain is now complete. He is the
humanistic intellectual alone in an alien and increasingly
hostile universe. For a time he contrives, armed with a

revolver and a whip, to maintain the vestiges of Moreau's authority, but he is unable to prevent the reversion to the creatures' original animal state. In particular, they lose the gift of speech: 'Can you imagine language, once clear-cut and exact, softening and guttering, losing shape and import, becoming mere lumps of sound again?' (21) (this is a significant detail, since Moreau had claimed that 'the great difference between man and monkey is in the larynx . . . in the incapacity to frame delicately different sound-symbols by which thought could be sustained') (14). But after Moreau's manipulations they are unable to return to a conventional animal form:

Of course these creatures did not decline into such beasts as the reader has seen in zoological gardens—into ordinary bears, wolves, tigers, oxen, swine, and apes. There was still something strange about each; in each Moreau had blended this animal with that; one perhaps was ursine chiefly, another feline chiefly, another bovine chiefly, but each was tainted with other creatures —a kind of generalized animalism appeared through the specific dispositions. And the dwindling shreds of the humanity still startled me every now and then, a momentary recrudescence of speech perhaps, an unexpected dexterity of the forefeet, a pitiful attempt to walk erect.

I too must have undergone strange changes. My clothes hung about me as yellow rags, through whose rents glowed the tanned skin. My hair grew long, and became matted together. I am told that even now my eyes have a strange brightness, a swift alertness of movement (21).

After several months, Prendick is virtually declining to the state of the other animals, and his life amongst them becomes increasingly precarious. One day he is menaced by a creature called the Hyaena-Swine which has lost all traces of humanity; he is able to shoot it, but thereby shows that he must now rely on physical not moral force in order to preserve himself. Prendick realizes that he must expect other such incidents, and that sooner or later he must succumb, since he has few cartridges left.

He is able to make his escape from the island in a fittingly macabre fashion. A boat drifts into the shore carrying two dead men (another detail perhaps taken from the *Narrative of Arthur Gordon Pym*). Prendick tips out the bodies, and after taking on some food and water sails away from the island. He drifts for three days, and is then picked up by a ship. His return to civilization recalls Gulliver's return at the end of the Fourth Book. Just as Gulliver had seen men as Yahoos, so Prendick sees them as humanized beasts:

I could not persuade myself that the men and women I met were not also another, still passably human, Beast People, animals half-wrought into the outward image of human souls, and that they would presently begin to revert, to show first this bestial mark and then that (22).

The Island of Dr Moreau, if my reading of it is correct, is a version of the 'island myth' which conveys a powerful and wholly imaginative response to the implications of Evolution. And this, I think, accounts for its generally hostile reception. One reviewer of the novel had spoken of 'a foul ambition to remake God's creatures by confusing and transfusing and remoulding human and animal organs so as to extinguish [*sic*] as far as possible the chasm which divides man from brute'.[24] One of the effects of Darwin, conceived in terms of the traditional religious world-picture, had been precisely to abolish 'the chasm which divides man from brute'. Wells's book shows us a world in which animals can be changed into men at the command of the quasi-divine scientist, and then, after his power has been removed, can be seen to regress to a distorted version of their original shape. There is no essential difference between man and animal, nothing which cannot be affected by surgical manipulation. This would certainly have been offensive to Wells's more traditionally minded readers; but at the same time, the romanticizing of Moreau, and his specific identification with the arbitrariness and indifference to suffering of what Huxley had called the 'cosmic process', would have offended scientifically inclined readers. And in either case, the stress on blood and the business of surgery would have added to the distaste. Wells's own attitude, as not infrequently in his early fiction and essays, was calculatedly ambiguous. Moreau is shown, in effect, as a monster who meets the fate he deserves, but at the same time Wells seems to make out as good a case for him as he can.

But there can be no doubt that *The Island of Dr Moreau* is a deeply pessimistic book, and its Swiftian view of human nature is not a mere literary exercise. Anthony West has remarked, 'What the book in fact expresses is a profound mistrust of human nature, and a doubt about the intellect's ability to contain it.' [25] When we compare this with the relative complacency of Wells's later utopian constructions, we have a measure of the change of attitude he was to undergo in the next few years. In *Evolution and Ethics*, Huxley had observed that Man had kept his ascendancy by the qualities of the ape and the tiger, but that in civilized society these were seen as defects.[26] *The Island of Dr Moreau* is a dramatization of the dilemma implicit in this statement.

3

In *The Invisible Man* Wells was to return to the blend of fantasy and everyday detail that he had employed in *The Wonderful Visit* and many of his short stories. In general, *The Invisible Man* was found much more acceptable by Wells's critics than *The Island of Dr Moreau*. It was published as a book in September 1897, though it had previously been serialized, in a rather shorter version, between June and August of that year in *Pearson's Weekly*. At the same time, *The War of the Worlds* was serialized in *Pearson's Magazine* from April to November 1897, and it is probable that this work was written, or at least started, before *The Invisible Man*, even though it was not published in book form until January 1898.[27] However, in terms of Wells's literary development *The Invisible Man* seems to fall naturally into place between *The Island of Dr Moreau* and *The War of the Worlds*: the latter work needs fuller and separate consideration. What is certain is that Wells gave *The Invisible Man* a good deal of rewriting before it was published, for he told an interviewer that an early draft of the story had totalled about 100,000 words before being cut down to only 55,000.[28] It seems to have been Wells's habit at this time to make very copious first drafts of his fiction, and then revise by making radical excisions. In fact, *The Invisible Man* is not wholly successful as a narrative, though it bears the marks of careful composition. It falls somewhere between the episodic manner of *The Wonderful Visit* and the more taut narrative structure of *The Time Machine* or *Moreau*. In particular, Griffin's lengthy recapitulation of his discovery and adventures—in Chapters 19–23—seems a somewhat clumsy device. Nevertheless, the central conception of the story, and Wells's handling of it, have been more than enough to justify its present position as a popular classic.

The theme of invisibility was, of course, an ancient folk-lore motif, and had been dealt with in a supernatural fashion from time to time by writers of romantic fiction: earlier nineteenth century examples include Maupassant's tale, 'Le Horla', and Fitzjames O'Brien's 'What Was It?' But Wells was probably the first writer to combine the traditional theme with a sober and plausible-seeming explanation drawn from contemporary physics and chemistry. As Clement Shorter wrote:

The cap which makes for the invisible is familiar enough in fairy tales. But Mr Wells has not obtained a smattering of science for naught. It was Huxley and Tyndall who made him possible, although both would have loathed his conclusions; and he gives us a fairy tale with a plausible scientific justification. The imagination is everything, the science is nothing; but the end of the century, which shares Mr Wells's smattering of South Kensington, prefers the two together; and I sympathize with the end of the century.[29]

The opening chapters of the novel, with the mysterious and grotesque stranger suddenly arriving in a small village, where he settles down, and indulges in curious scientific experiments, are generally reminiscent of the opening of *The Chronic Argonauts*. Wells seems to have been consciously using some of this material and there are one or two verbal parallels. Thus, when Nebogipfel's scientific apparatus is delivered to the Manse it includes 'jars and phials labelled in black and scarlet—POISON', while the mighty assortment of bottles that Griffin unpacks in the 'Coach and Horses' at Iping includes 'little fat bottles containing powders, small and slender bottles containing coloured and white fluids, fluted blue bottles labelled *poison*. . . .'(3) As I have already argued, Nebogipfel, Moreau and Griffin are all variants of a single type, the scientist-as-alchemist, who is not disinterestedly concerned with knowledge for its own sake, but pursues it as a means of obtaining power. A similar figure can also be found in Wells's short story, 'The Diamond Maker'. But if Nebogipfel and Griffin are related types, the environments in which they start their operations are very different. The Carnarvonshire country people in *The Chronic Argonauts* are all intensely superstitious, only too ready to believe that the visitor is a warlock, whereas Wells says of the villagers in *The Invisible Man*, 'the Sussex peasants are perhaps the most matter-of-fact people under the sun' (7). Indeed, much of the comedy of the book comes from the villagers' assumption that Griffin, extraordinary though he is, is an absurd rather than a terrifying figure. One of them considers that he is a 'piebald'—'black here and white there —in patches. And he's ashamed of it. He's a kind of half-breed, and the colour's come off patchy instead of mixing' (3). Another of them accepts this theory, and considers that 'if he chose to show enself at fairs he'd make a fortune in no time' (4). Others regard him as a harmless lunatic.

Wells here is not merely indulging in an agreeable vein of humour for its own sake, but is imaginatively reducing the stature of the stranger. These passages implicitly anticipate those at the end of the book in which Griffin becomes an actual outcast from society. Even when he becomes violent and homicidal we cannot forget that he is also absurd. And here perhaps is the main difference between Griffin—considered in context—and Nebogipfel and Moreau. In the first part of the story Griffin is not allowed to remain at the imaginative centre of interest. We see him, not directly as weird or terrifying, but through the matter-of-fact eyes of the Iping villagers, who are very much aware of his preposterous elements. And he has to share the interest with the comedy of village life that Wells so brilliantly presents. In *The Wonderful Visit* Wells's sympathy with village life was merely implicit, since it ran counter to his overt satirical intentions, but in *The Invisible Man* (which is set in the same part of Sussex, sharing many of the same imaginary place-names) the sympathy and affection are quite explicit. Wells vividly conveys the *feel* of a Sussex village on a fine Whit Monday in the nineties:

Haysman's meadow was gay with a tent, in which Mrs Bunting and other ladies were preparing tea, while without the Sunday school children ran races and played games under the noisy guidance of the curate and the Misses Cuss and Sackbut. No doubt there was a slight uneasiness in the air, but people for the most part had the sense to conceal whatever imaginative qualms they experienced. On the village green an inclined string, down which, clinging the while to a pulley-swung handle, one could be hurled violently against a sack at the other end, came in for considerable favour among the adolescent, as also did the swings and the coconut-shies. There was also promenading, and the steam organ attached to a small roundabout filled the air with a pungent flavour of oil and with equally pungent music. Members of the club, who had attended church in the morning, were splendid in badges of pink and green, and some of the gayer minded had also adorned their bowler hats with brilliant coloured favours of ribbon. Old Fletcher, whose conceptions of holiday-making were severe, was visible through the jasmine about his window or through the open door (whichever way you chose to look) poised delicately on a plank supported on two chairs, and whitewashing the ceiling of his front room (10).

The early chapters of *The Invisible Man*, in my opinion, contain some of Wells's finest social comedy, showing to full advantage his perception of topographical detail and his acute ear for vernacular dialogue: they anticipate such later sustained comedies as *Kipps* and *The History of Mr Polly*. The tramp, Mr Thomas Marvell, though a development of the 'Philosophical Tramp' who appears in *The Wonderful Visit*, is a more genial and fully rounded character, and is one of Wells's most successful neo-Dickensian creations.

The significance of *The Invisible Man* in terms of Wells's fictional development is that, for the first time in his romances, we are shown a recognizable society in being which engages our sympathy and interest for its own sake. Instead of seeing a society, albeit a small one, through the eyes of a strange visitor, as in *The Wonderful Visit*, we see the strange visitor—to begin with—through the eyes of the society. And, as Wells emphasizes, it is a smug, settled and apparently prosperous little community. Later, Griffin is to disturb its peace in the farcical events of Whit Monday when he goes berserk and inflicts widespread—if minor—damage to property and injury to its inhabitants. Thematically, *The Invisible Man* relates those romances in which the interest is centred in the heuristic perceptions of a single figure—the Time Traveller, the Angel, Prendick—to *The War of the Worlds*, where attention is focused on society as a whole as it is subject to the unwelcome attentions of not one but a multitude of alien visitants.

As the narrative develops, following the events of Whit Monday, we become more concerned with Griffin himself, particularly when he gives his autobiographical account to Dr Kemp at Burdock. Kemp can be seen as a personification of the 'normal' or orthodox scientist, a steadfast sober investigator, quietly working for his F.R.S., in marked contrast to the romantic extravagance of Griffin. Kemp, in short, stands for South Kensington as against Frankenstein. He is also, it is interesting to note, a pragmatist in ethics. Though Kemp has given Griffin his word that he will be safe in his house, he nevertheless betrays him to the police when he realizes Griffin's maniacal proclivities: ' "For instance, would it be a breach of faith if—No" '(18). Griffin, on the other hand, manifests the kind of revolutionary attitude to ethical questions that we have previously seen in Moreau, and which is also apparent in the 'Diamond Maker'. He tells Kemp that in order to get money for his research he had stolen from his father, and ' "The money was not his, and he shot himself" '(19). He feels no remorse for this, and he goes on to remark:

I did not feel a bit sorry for my father. He seemed to me to be the victim of his own foolish sentimentality. The current cant required my attendance at his funeral, but it was really not my affair . . . (20)

As the novel develops Griffin becomes increasingly alienated, both from his environment and from the reader. The process that began in the opening chapters, when he was shown as a ridiculous figure, is accentuated when Griffin reveals in his own words the extent of his homicidal potentialities.

And it is killing we must do, Kemp. . . . Not wanton killing, but a judicious slaying. The point is: They know there is an Invisible Man . . . and that Invisible Man, Kemp, must now establish a Reign of Terror. Yes; no doubt it's startling, but I mean it. A Reign of Terror. He must take some town, like your Burdock, and terrify and dominate it. He must issue his orders. He can do that in a thousand ways—scraps of paper thrust under doors would suffice. And all who disobey his orders he must kill, and kill all who would defend them (24).

Similarly, Griffin's own actions underline his increasing alienation. From the mere violent horseplay at Iping on Whit Monday he goes on to the murder of Mr Wicksteed and the final furious onslaught on Kemp. By the end of the book he appears to be insane.

The final pages of the story which describe how Griffin is killed by a navvy with a spade, and, once dead, gradually returns to visibility, contains some of Wells's most vivid writing. Here the Invisible Man is neither absurd nor terrifying, but simply pathetic:

Some one brought a sheet from the 'Jolly Cricketers', and having covered him, they carried him into that house. And there, on a shabby bed in a tawdry, ill-lighted bedroom, ended the strange experiment of the Invisible Man (28).

It is arguable that the transitions in mood in *The Invisible Man* are too abrupt, and that the attempted combination, as it were, of Thurber and Kafka, is ultimately unsatisfactory. Yet, as I have suggested, all the changes in feeling with which Griffin is associated do point in one direction: namely, that of making him seem more and more an outcast from the kind of everyday society whose weight and solidity Wells is at such pains to establish. One contemporary reviewer wrote of the book:

The tragedy is always on the brink of farce until we reach the last page and a piece of wholly pathetic tragedy. The hunted terror of society is caught at last, and most pitiful is the re-entry he makes into the visible world he left so boldly.[30]

One is reminded here of the concept of 'tragic farce' that T. S. Eliot applied to Marlowe's *Jew of Malta*,[31] and this certainly seems as good a description as any of *The Invisible Man*: Griffin, like Barabas, is both farcical and murderous.

It is certainly possible, as Norman Nicholson has suggested, to take *The Invisible Man* as a simple manifestation of the traditional myth of invisibility, of the fear of 'things that go bump in the night', of that which can be apprehended but not seen.[32] But the story has more particular meanings than this. For instance, it is not difficult to draw an ironic moral from Griffin's adventures. Once he has made himself invisible, he is filled with a sense of power:

I was invisible, and I was only just beginning to realize the extraordinary advantage my invisibility gave me. My head was already teeming with plans of all the wild and wonderful things I had now impunity to do (20).

But in the event he becomes a helpless creature, naked in January on the streets of London, sniffed at by dogs, with children tracking his footprints, and having to take ignominious refuge in a department store. (Although Griffin remarks, 'Foolish as it seems to me now, I had not reckoned that, transparent or not, I was still amenable to the weather and all its consequences,' it seems a serious flaw in Wells's narrative—though necessary for the 'plot'—that Griffin so inexplicably neglected to make his clothes invisible, and thus had to go out naked.) In this reading, *The Invisible Man* becomes a moral story of hubris and its inevitable downfall.

However, this interpretation needs to be modified—or deepened—by the knowledge that Griffin is not merely a private and isolated individual, but does in some sense stand for the possibilities of scientific achievement, or at least for Wells's romantic apprehension of these possibilities. Thus Griffin's punishment must be seen as a rebuke for the pretensions of science. And this was the view of Clement Shorter, in the review from which I have already quoted: 'Scientific research is indeed vanity if we are to accept Mr Wells as a guide.' As I have tried to show, Wells in his early years was far from being an unquestioning positivist. His attitude to science was, in fact, sceptical where it was not ambiguous. In *Moreau* we are shown the *possibilities* of science without in any way being convinced that these are necessarily beneficial. And something similar is true of *The Invisible Man*. One can take this interpretation further and point out that Griffin is not only Wells's last version of the romantic scientist of the Frankenstein type, but also his most fully realized. In this novel Wells seems to have brought the type to final realization before imaginatively casting him out of his consciousness. Conceived in strictly mythical terms, Griffin, at the point of his death, has become a scapegoat figure hunted out of society: it is perhaps not altogether fanciful to suppose that what is being 'cast out' is not merely the dangerous pretensions of contemporary science, but also the young Wells's own identification with a highly romanticized kind of scientist-magician, first apparent in the aspirations of Nebogipfel. The point is underlined by the introduction into the story of the calm and pragmatic figure of the 'orthodox' scientist, Dr Kemp.

It is illuminating to compare *The Invisible Man* with the more ambitious but much less successful romance, *The Food of the Gods*, published in 1904. Here we find a basic imaginative incoherence arising from an unresolved conflict between mistrust of scientific possibilities and a whole-hearted acceptance of these possibilities. At the beginning of the novel our sympathies are engaged by the world of ordinary humanity which is being upset by the monstrous products of scientific research—this is very apparent in the vividly rendered fight against the giant rats at the Experimental Farm. Yet about half-way through the book there is a fatal change in the direction of sympathy—no doubt deliberately introduced by Wells for didactic purposes—and at the conclusion we are supposed to be on the side of the Giants, who represent the Future, against the puny humanity of the present day: by this point, as Chesterton remarked, the book 'is the tale of "Jack the Giant-killer" told from the point of view of the giant.'[33] By the early years of this century Wells's utopian and positivist convictions were coming increasingly to dominate his earlier intellectual scepticism and his imaginative attachment to the traditional patterns of southern English life. Wells was certainly aware of this conflict; in the twenties he wrote of himself: 'Temperamentally he is egotistic and romantic, intellectually he is clearly aware that the egotistic and romantic must go.'[34]

But in 1897 this conflict between the artist and the prophet was still only potential, and *The Invisible Man* is a fundamentally homogeneous book, despite its superficial variety of moods. Thematically it can be seen as marking the end of the earliest phase of Wells's romances, which embodies in various ways an individualistic preoccupation with the romantic scientist, whether he was seen as Nebogipfel, the

Time Traveller, Moreau or Griffin. For a final judgment on *The Invisible Man* one cannot do better than quote the remarks that Joseph Conrad made in a letter to Wells of December 1898:

Frankly—it is uncommonly fine. One can always *see* a lot in your work—there is always a 'beyond' to your books—but into this (with due regard to theme and length) you've managed to put an amazing quantity of effects. If it just misses being tremendous, it is because you didn't make it so—and if you didn't, there isn't a man in England who could.[35]

CHAPTER V

'THE WAR OF THE WORLDS'

IN my opinion, *The War of the Worlds* is, after *The Time
Machine*, Wells's finest piece of sustained imaginative writing. A similarly high opinion of it was held by several contemporary readers. One reviewer considered that it was 'the
best story he has yet produced',[1] and another wrote 'Mr
Wells has done good work before, but nothing quite so
fine as this'.[2] The *Spectator* devoted a long and very favourable review to the novel, comparing it with Defoe's *Journal
of the Plague Year*, as well as making the more customary
comparisons with Poe and Swift.[3] Clement Shorter in the
Bookman was admiring, though he regretted Wells's continued pessimism.[4] The *Athenaeum*, on the other hand,
which treated Wells's books in a systematically patronizing
way, was a dissenting voice, and complained that there was
'too much of the young man from Clapham attitude' about
it.[5]

Like *The Invisible Man*, *The War of the Worlds* embodies a
topic of considerable antiquity. From Lucian onwards,
imaginative writers had considered the possibility that the
Moon—or other celestial bodies—might be inhabited.[6]
Wells himself had certainly been interested in the idea from
his college days onwards. On 19 October 1888 he had spoken
to the Debating Society at the Royal College of Science on
the question, 'Are the Planets Habitable?' and he concluded
that 'there was every reason to suppose that the surface of
Mars was occupied by living beings'.[7] In 1896 Wells returned

to the question in an unsigned article, 'Intelligence on Mars', published in the *Saturday Review* on 4th April of that year. This concluded that even if Mars were inhabited by living beings, there need not be anything in common between their intelligence and ours. Historically, *The War of the Worlds* can be considered as the forerunner of much subsequent science fiction. Yet its central interest comes not from its mere treatment of the theme of interplanetary travel, as others had done before, but from the way in which Wells presents an image of human society as the passive victim of extraterrestrial invaders. In 1920 Wells wrote of the book:

The book was begotten by a remark of my brother Frank. We were walking together through some particularly peaceful Surrey scenery. 'Suppose some beings from another planet were to drop out of the sky suddenly,' said he, 'and begin laying about them here!' Perhaps we had been talking of the discovery of Tasmania by the Europeans—a very frightful disaster for the native Tasmanians! I forget. But that was the point of departure.

In those days I was writing short stories, and the particular sort of short story that amused me most to do was the vivid realization of some disregarded possibility in such a way as to comment on the false securities and fatuous self-satisfaction of the everyday life—as we knew it then. Because in those days the conviction that history had settled down to a sort of jog-trot comedy was very widespread indeed. Tragedy, people thought, had gone out of human life for ever. A few of us were trying to point out the obvious possibilities of flying, of great guns, of poison gas, and so forth in presently making life uncomfortable if some sort of world peace was not assured, but the books we wrote were regarded as the silliest of imaginative gymnastics. Well, the world knows better now.

The technical interest of a story like *The War of the Worlds* lies in the attempt to keep everything within the bounds of possibility. And the value of the story to me lies in this, that from first to last there is nothing in it that is impossible.[8]

One must discount here Wells's customary tendency to make his early work seem retrospectively more didactic than it actually was. In fact, as he himself admitted some years later, his romances were much more works of pure imagination and less concerned with actual possibilities than the fiction of Verne. However, as he says, there is much less that is manifestly impossible in *The War of the Worlds* than in the other romances, and some of the book's power undoubtedly comes from this fact. It can certainly be read as a 'comment on the false securities and fatuous self-satisfaction of the everyday life', though in a less direct sense than Wells intended.

The War of the Worlds lacks the comedy and sense of vivid characterization that mark the first part of *The Invisible Man*, but there is the same tangible sense of place, and the setting for the Martian invasion is rendered with extraordinary topographical detail and solidity. In 1895-6 Wells was living at Woking and in his autobiography he describes how he learnt to ride a bicycle there: 'Later on I wheeled about the district marking down suitable places and people for destruction by my Martians.'[9] In a letter to Elizabeth Healey he wrote:

I'm doing the dearest little serial for Pearson's new magazine, in which I completely wreck and destroy Woking—killing my neighbours in painful and eccentric ways—then proceed via Kingston and Richmond to London, which I sack, selecting South Kensington for feats of peculiar atrocity.[10]

In *The War of the Worlds* the Martians establish the 'Reign of Terror' that the Invisible Man could only dream of—and on an infinitely larger scale. The quotation shows the ease with which Wells's imagination ran to images of mutilation and violence, already evident from *The Island of Dr Moreau* and *The Time Machine*. Even in the peaceful 'Holiday Adventure', *The Wheels of Chance*, Mr Hoopdriver can dream in these terms: 'Nearer, nearer! It was fearful! and in another moment the houses were cracking like nuts, and the blood of the inhabitants squirting this way and that!' (12).

The structure of *The War of the Worlds*, like that of *The Invisible Man*, is not without its flaws. The division of the narrative between the philosopher in Woking and his brother, the medical student, in London is awkward, though it is to some extent justified in practice since it enables Wells to combine the largeness of design that he was obviously seeking with the immediacy of first-person narration. Nevertheless, one is rather disconcerted by the abruptness with which the brother and the two ladies he is escorting are dropped from the story after the events of Book I, Chapter 17. The expendability of the narrative source emphasizes that for the first time in Wells's early romances the stress is placed on society rather than on any individual; hence, too, the total lack of any interest in characterization, if we except the stock anti-clerical caricature of the curate. We are concerned exclusively with events.

The Time Machine, it is true, had on one level dealt with society, for it had presented a symbolic image drawn from certain observable tendencies in contemporary society. But one saw the wholly imaginary world of 802701 through the eyes of the Traveller, and became aware of it exclusively in terms of his perceptions and attempted explanations. In *The War of the Worlds* the narrator is far less obtrusive, and we are presented with the physical realities of contemporary society, and the events that impinge upon them, in purely documentary terms and in an intensely visual fashion that frequently anticipates cinematic techniques. One may consider, for instance, the passage in which the story-teller returns by night to his house at Woking, after taking his wife and servant to Leatherhead, and sees from an upstairs window the fires that the Martians have started in the town below:

I closed the door noiselessly and crept towards the window. As I did so, the view opened out until, on the one hand, it reached to the houses about Woking Station, and on the other to the charred and blackened pine-woods of Byfleet. There was a light down below the hill, on the railway, near the arch, and several of the houses along the Maybury road and the streets near the station were glowing ruins. The light upon the railway puzzled me at first; there was a black heap and a vivid glare, and to the right of that a row of yellow oblongs. Then I perceived this was a wrecked train, the fore part smashed and on fire, the hinder carriages still upon the rails (I. 11).

This pinning of events to a detailed topographical background (and ideally one should read the opening chapters of *The War of the Worlds* with a map of West Surrey by one's side) is certainly a simple and obvious device, but in context it is extraordinarily effective, and the effect is cumulative. One sees in minute detail the bourgeois world of Southern England in the late nineties at the precise moment of its imagined destruction. Combined with this accuracy of physical observation is an equally precise sense of time, of the hour-by-hour sequence of events; the two elements together produce the feeling of intolerably mounting tension which dominates the first part of the book:

About three o'clock there began the thud of a gun at measured intervals from Chertsey or Addlestone. I learnt that the smouldering pine-wood into which the second cylinder had fallen was being shelled, in the hope of destroying that object before it opened. It was only about five, however, that a field-gun reached Chobham for use against the first body of Martians.

About six in the evening, as I sat at tea with my wife in the summer-house talking vigorously about the battle that was lowering upon us, I heard a muffled detonation from the common, and immediately after a gust of firing. Close on the heels of that came a violent, rattling crash, quite close to us, that shook the ground; and, starting out upon the lawn, I saw the tops of the trees about the Oriental College burst into smoky red flame, and the tower of the little church beside it slide down into ruin. The pinnacle of the mosque had vanished, and the roof-line of the college itself looked as if a hundred-ton gun had been at work upon it. One of our chimneys cracked as if a shot had hit it, flew, and the piece of it came clattering down the tiles and made a heap of broken red fragments upon the flower-bed by my study window.

I and my wife stood amazed. Then I realized that the crest of Maybury Hill must be within range of the Martians' Heat-Ray now that the college was cleared out of the way (I. 9).

The effect is continued, on a much larger scale, in the account of the adventures of the narrator's brother in London as the news of the Martians gradually reaches the capital. Here we are given a step by step report on the break-up of Metropolitan society. On Saturday morning, over twenty-four hours after the arrival of the first Martian cylinder on Horsell Common, the London papers contain brief and vaguely-worded reports of the events there. The afternoon papers report the movement of troops about the common, and the burning of the pinewoods between Woking and Weybridge; then at eight in the evening the *St James's Gazette* announces that telegraphic communication has been cut. At Waterloo, later that night, the narrator's brother finds that no trains are running to Woking, though it is merely assumed that a local breakdown has occurred. In the Sunday morning papers there are fresh reports of the destruction at Woking, but no-one in London seems very disturbed. As the day advances other railway lines into

Surrey are cut and fighting is reported from Weybridge. There is still no general panic, but soon day trippers begin returning from Richmond, Putney and Kingston, with reports of gun-fire and refugees. Then the Sunday excursionists return from Barnes, Wimbledon, Richmond Park, and Kew 'at unnaturally early hours; but not a soul had anything but vague hearsay to tell of' (I. 14). By five o'clock heavy guns are being transported to defend the south-western approaches to London. In the early evening fuller reports come in of the Martians and their machines, and the first refugees from West Surrey are seen on the streets of London. Then, 'About eight o'clock a noise of heavy firing was distinctly audible all over the south of London' (I. 14). Later in the evening, more refugees arrive, and further firing is heard.

In the small hours of Monday morning the narrator's brother is awakened by the police: ' "They are coming!" bawled a policeman, hammering at the door: "the Martians are coming!" and hurried to the next door' (I. 14). He gets up and finds that people are already fleeing the Martians and the 'Black Smoke'. 'London, which had gone to bed on Sunday night stupid and inert, was awakened in the small hours of Monday morning to a vivid sense of danger.'

The opening of Book I, Chapter 16, 'The Exodus from London', describes the ensuing panic, and the break-up of the social organism here reaches its appalling climax:

So you understand the roaring wave of fear that swept through the greatest city in the world just as Monday was dawning—the stream of flight rising swiftly to a torrent, lashing in a foaming tumult round the railway-stations, banked up into a horrible struggle about the shipping in the Thames, and hurrying by every available channel northward and eastward. By ten o'clock the police organization, and by mid-day even the railway organizations, were losing coherency, losing shape and efficiency, guttering, softening, running at last in that swift liquefaction of the social body.

All the railway lines north of the Thames and the South-Eastern people at Cannon Street had been warned by midnight on Sunday, and trains were being filled, people were fighting savagely for standing room in the carriages, even at two o'clock. By three people were being trampled and crushed even in Bishopsgate street; a couple of hundred yards or more from Liverpool Street Station revolvers were fired, people stabbed, and the policemen who had been sent to direct the traffic, exhausted and infuriated, were breaking the heads of the people they were called out to protect.

And as the day advanced and the engine-drivers and stokers refused to return to London, the pressure of the flight drove the people in an ever-thickening multitude away from the stations and along the northward-running roads. By mid-day a Martian had been seen at Barnes, and a cloud of slowly sinking black vapour drove along the Thames and across the flats of Lambeth, cutting off all escape over the bridges in its sluggish advance. Another bank drove over Ealing, and surrounded a little island of survivors on Castle Hill, alive, but unable to escape.

Wells here can be seen at his most prophetic, for the events he describes—first the rumours and then the reality of invasion, followed by panic—have become familiar in the history of the twentieth century. But these scenes are all the more remarkable for being written out of pure imagination: they remind one of the similar gift displayed by Wells's friend, Stephen Crane, in the writing of *The Red Badge of Courage*. The novel reaches its imaginative peak in the chapter headed 'Dead London' (Book II, Chapter 8), where the narrator slowly makes his way into the completely dead and deserted city via the south-western suburbs. At South Kensington he hears a distant howling sound—'It was a sobbing alternation of two notes, "Ulla, ulla, ulla, ulla," keeping on perpetually' and the pages in which the narrator tracks it to its source across the dead city, through Exhibition Road, Hyde Park, Oxford Street, and Regent's Park, are perhaps the most memorable in the book. As the *Saturday Review* critic wrote:

The picture of the last Martian, in its bewildered agony, howling in the twilight from the summit of Primrose Hill over a silent and devastated London, is one of the most effective which we have met for years. We shall long hear 'Ulla! ulla!' echoing in our dreams.[11]

Finally the Martian invaders are defeated by the bacteria to which human beings are immune, but against which the Martians have no resistance. Yet though the novel ends on a note of qualified hope for humanity (and even the narrator's wife is restored to him), the book provides in its entirety an image of destruction rather than any very strong imaginative assurance of regeneration.

The theme of *The War of the Worlds*, the physical destruction of society, or at least the dissolution of the social order, was one of the dominant preoccupations of the *fin de siècle* period. We have already seen this *fin du globe* myth expressed in the final vision of the dying world in *The Time Machine*, which is essentially *fin de siècle* in Nordau's sense. Equally so is a brief but very important early essay by Wells, 'The Extinction of Man', originally published in the *Pall Mall Gazette* on 23 September 1894.[12] The tone of the piece is lightly ironical, but there is no doubt that, in Nordau's words, 'the prevalent feeling is that of imminent perdition and extinction'. Wells discusses the various ways in which the end of the human race might come about. Man might one day succumb to a greatly enlarged breed of land-crab, or to unknown sea-monsters, or a new kind of predatory ant, or simply to some previously unknown disease. This essay is interesting since it contains several suggestions subsequently developed in Wells's fiction: the land-crabs appear in *The Time Machine*, the sea-monsters in 'The Sea Raiders', and the ants in 'The Empire of the Ants'. But the central significance of 'The Extinction of Man' is, I think, its decidedly *fin de siècle* attitude to the future of Humanity. The final paragraph runs thus:

No; man's complacent assumption of the future is too confident. We think, because things have been easy for mankind as a whole for a generation or so, we are going on to perfect comfort and security in the future. We think that we shall always go to work at ten and leave off at four and have dinner at seven for ever and ever. But these four suggestions out of a host of others must surely do a little against this complacency. Even now, for all we can tell, the coming terror may be crouching for its spring and the fall of humanity be at hand. In the case of every other pre-dominant animal the world has ever seen, I repeat, the hour of its complete ascendency has been the eve of its complete overthrow. But if some poor story-writing man ventures to figure this sober probability in a tale, not a reviewer in London but will tell him his theme is the utterly impossible. And when the thing happens, one may doubt if even then one will get the recognition one deserves.[13]

This would certainly have been grist to Nordau's mill: at the same time it obviously anticipates the underlying theme of *The War of the Worlds*. This theme is, in fact, implicit in the carefully calculated opening paragraph of the novel, which continues both the tone and the arguments of 'The Extinction of Man':

No one would have believed, in the last years of the nineteenth century, that human affairs were being watched keenly and closely by intelligences greater than man's and yet as mortal as his own; that as men busied themselves about their affairs they were scrutinized and studied, perhaps almost as narrowly as a man with a microscope might scrutinize the transient creatures that swarm and multiply in a drop of water. With infinite complacency men went to and fro over this globe about their little affairs, serene in their assurance of their empire over matter. It is possible that the infusoria under the microscope do the same. No one gave a thought to the older worlds of space as sources of human danger, or thought of them only to dismiss the idea of life upon them as impossible or improbable. It is curious to recall some of the mental habits of those departed days. At most, terrestrial men fancied there might be other men upon Mars, perhaps inferior to themselves and ready to welcome a missionary enterprise. Yet, across the gulf of space, minds that are to our minds as ours are to those of the beasts that perish, intellects vast and cool and unsympathetic, regarded this earth with envious eyes, and slowly and surely drew their plans against us. And early in the twentieth century came the great disillusionment.

As we have seen, Wells had been interested for several years in the possibility of life on Mars, and the subject seems to have been much discussed in the early nineties (the first volume of Camille Flammarion's monumental work, *La Planète Mars*, had appeared in 1892), so the Martians made a convenient and plausible superhuman adversary for mankind. But in a sense they can be seen as a projection of Wells's *fin de siècle* forebodings about the future, combined with the desire to *épater le bourgeois* already apparent in *Moreau*. Furthermore, they are themselves an image of the possible future of humanity with evident affinities with Wells's own 'Man of the Year Million'. This is made explicit in Chapter 2 of Book II of *The War of the Worlds*, where Wells ironically alludes to his own early essay (see above, page 38): he continues:

To me it is quite credible that the Martians may be descended from beings not unlike ourselves, by a gradual development of brain and hands (the latter giving rise to two bunches of delicate tentacles at last) at the expense of the rest of the body. Without the body, the brain would of course become a more selfish intelligence, without any of the emotional substratum of the human being.

The Martians, in short, embody the kind of 'Superman' ideal that both Moreau and Griffin aspired to. *The War of the Worlds* can be seen, then, as continuing the Darwinian preoccupation of *The Time Machine* and *Moreau*, even though its major stress is sociological. Wells was to return to the theme of dissolution, and the near-destruction of society, in his short story, 'The Star'.

But there is a further sense in which *The War of the Worlds* is pre-eminently a work of its time. It is worth recalling that the novel first appeared as a magazine serial in 1897, the year of the second Victorian jubilee, when national complacency and self-righteousness had reached such a peak that even Kipling felt obliged to deliver a warning in his 'Recessional'. In one sense the novel is about Imperialism in its most oppressive aspects simply by imagining the contemporary English as its victims:

The Tasmanians, in spite of their human likeness, were entirely swept out of existence in a war of extermination waged by European immigrants in the space of fifty years. Are we such apostles of mercy as to complain if the Martians warred in the same spirit? (I. 1).

On the one hand, *The War of the Worlds* can be seen as expressing a certain guilty conscience about imperialism, and on the other as dramatizing the fear of invasion that was an intermittent preoccupation of English society in the final decades of the last century. The word 'War' in its title would have had a significance then which is now lost, and it is revealing to consider Wells's novel in the context of the innumerable books and pamphlets which, from about 1870 onward, described imaginary future wars, many of them involving the invasion of England followed by—in some cases—national defeat and humiliation at the hands of a foreign enemy—usually either the French or the Germans.[14] Most of these works are of minimal literary interest, and *The War of the Worlds* is immediately distinguished from them by its greater imaginative intensity and technical superiority, qualities which have ensured its survival while superficially similar contemporary works have been forgotten. Many of these war stories had a didactic intention: the authors, often professional soldiers, wished to expose national unpreparedness and to warn of the fate that might befall the country if its defences were not put in order. Yet they can also be seen as expressing *fin de siècle* forebodings about the future, and as manifestations—in the more pessimistic examples—of the *fin du globe* mood. Indeed, the historian Halévy has not hesitated to describe certain aspects of British national life—and particularly foreign policy—in this period as 'decadent':

... whatever the improvements made in her national institutions, England felt an increasingly powerful conviction that her vitality was less than that of certain other nations, and that if she was progressing, her rate of progress was less rapid than theirs— that is to say, if not absolutely, at least relatively to her rivals, she was declining. It was this loss of confidence which explains the far-reaching change in her foreign policy which took place towards the end of the nineteenth century.[15]

Whatever Wells's intentions in this respect may have been, there can be no doubt that *The War of the Worlds* would have played upon existing fears of foreign invasion, and so embodies a very prevalent *fin de siècle* myth.

In general, the theme of the novel is stated obliquely, and does not obtrude discursively through the surface of the narrative: it appears in the images which the narrative presents. The physical destruction wrought to Victorian society in Jubilee year has obvious metaphorical implications, and can certainly be taken as standing for a potential moral dissolution. The scenes of the 'swift liquefaction of the social body' in the mass exodus from London point in this direction, and at the same time recall the comparable dissolution of the animal body that was the central preoccupation of *Moreau*. Again, when the philosopher-narrator, who has previously lived a very comfortable bourgeois life, is forced to spend a fortnight hiding in a ruined house in the company of the mad curate, living on scraps, it is not difficult to see that an ironic comment is being made about the habitual assumptions of everyday life. Nevertheless, *The War of the Worlds* is by no means an overtly didactic work and the simple vigour of its narrative has been sufficient to keep it popular with a variety of readers for over sixty years. Yet at one point near the end of the book Wells does allow himself the luxury of presenting ideas for their own sake. This is in Chapter 7 of Book II, 'The Man on Putney Hill', in which the narrator encounters the 'Artilleryman'. This character has so far succeeded in eluding the Martians and is determined to continue doing so; men must adapt themselves to the new conditions, he says, and prepare to live a kind of underground life. But civilization as it has so far existed is finished, he says, and man must recognize the fact:

'Cities, nations, civilization, progress—it's all over. That game's up. We're beat.'
'But if that is so, what is there to live for:'
The artilleryman looked at me for a moment.
'There won't be any more blessed concerts for a million years or so; there won't be any Royal Academy of Arts, and no nice little feeds at restaurants. If it's amusement you're after, I reckon

the game is up. If you've got any drawing-room manners, or a dislike to eating peas with a knife, or dropping aitches, you'd better chuck 'em away. They ain't no further use.'

'You mean——'

'I mean that men like me are going on living—for the sake of the breed. I tell you, I'm grim set on living. And, if I'm not mistaken, you'll show what insides *you've* got, too, before long. We aren't going to be exterminated. And I don't mean to be caught, either, and tamed and fattened and bred like a thundering ox . . .'

Most men, he says, are fit for nothing but to be preyed on by the Martians—'those damn little clerks that used to live down *that* way', and 'the bar-loafers, and mashers, and singers'. He says of them: 'Well, the Martians will just be a god-send to these. Nice roomy cages, fattening food, careful breeding, no worry.' But the real men, those of superior physical and mental powers, must band together and live underground, and perhaps one day find a way of overcoming the Martians:

And we form a band—able-bodied, clean-minded men. We're not going to pick up any rubbish that drifts in. Weaklings go out again. . . . Those who stop, obey orders. Able-bodied, clean-minded women we want also—mothers and teachers. No lackadaisical ladies—no blasted rolling eyes. We can't have anything weak or silly. Life is real again, and the useless and cumbersome and mischievous have to die. They ought to die. They ought to be willing to die. It's a sort of disloyalty, after all, to live and taint the race. And they can't be happy. Moreover, dying's none so dreadful;—it's the funking that makes it bad (II. 7).

The Artilleryman, in fact, positively welcomes the destruction of contemporary society, and his views about the élite who are going to ensure the continuance of humanity curiously anticipate some of the more idealistic doctrines of

European fascism (a more immediate cross-reference can perhaps be made to Kipling). In terms of Wells's own subsequent development we have here the first suggestion of the need for an intellectual and physical élite which was increasingly to dominate his sociological thinking, and which received its most systematic expression in the Samurai of *A Modern Utopia*. It is significant that the chapter in which the Artilleryman appears is lacking in the serialized version of the novel, and so presumably was deliberately inserted by Wells before the novel appeared in permanent form. Nor can there be any doubt that the Artilleryman's views are those of Wells himself, or at least that they are based on ideas which Wells was prepared to consider very seriously, if in a speculative fashion. For evidence, one can turn to some passages in an essay on Gissing that Wells published in August 1897, when *The War of the Worlds* was being serialized. There he speaks of:

a change that is sweeping over the minds of thousands of educated men. It is the discovery of the insufficiency of the cultivated life and its necessary insincerities; it is a return to the essential, to honourable struggle as the epic factor in life, to children as the matter of morality and the sanction of the securities of civilization.[16]

The deliberate introduction of these ideas in *The War of the Worlds* is, as it were, the thin end of the didactic wedge that within a few years was to transform Wells from an artist into a prophet. But in the context of the narrative Wells ironically redresses the balance by making his narrator perceive, within a few pages, that the Artilleryman is a complete idler who has neither the intention nor the ability to put his plans into effect.

Whereas *The Time Machine* is organized poetically, *The War of the Worlds* employs the methods of minute documentary realism; but both have a mythical significance. Before long, however, Wells was to consider fiction not as a means of dramatizing and imaginatively enacting ideas, but simply of discussing them.

CHAPTER VI

'WHEN THE SLEEPER WAKES' AND
'THE FIRST MEN IN THE MOON'

I

In the summer of 1897, when he was at work on *Love and Mr Lewisham*, Wells told an interviewer, 'I am also thinking of another scientific romance of *The Time Machine* and *War of the Worlds* type.'[1] This new romance was to be *When the Sleeper Wakes*, which was written during the winter of 1897–8. Wells recognized that it was a rather botched piece of work, and took the opportunity to revise it before the novel was reissued in 1910 under the title of *The Sleeper Awakes*. As early as 1903 he had written that *When the Sleeper Wakes* would shortly be reissued 'in a greatly revised form',[2] but the changes in the new edition, when it finally appeared, were not radical: cuts had been made in the text totalling about 6,000 words, mainly in the later chapters, and there were a number of minor verbal changes. By 1910 Wells felt that the original conception of the book was too remote for it to be very much altered.[3] Yet even if one admits that the novel suffered from being finished in a hurry, it is doubtful whether more time spent on the conclusion would have made it a basically better book. Although Wells claimed that *When the Sleeper Wakes* was a 'scientific romance of *The Time Machine* and *War of the Worlds* type', the difference in imaginative intensity and artistic coherence between it and those works is immediately apparent. Nor is this decline in quality in any way remarkable; during the years

1894–7 Wells had produced without any intermission a series of romances, a realistic novel, and innumerable short stories and essays, and it was only to be expected that his imagination would show signs of flagging. The critical reception of the novel was generally unfavourable and some reviewers were severe in their comments: the *Speaker* declared that it 'never soars above the commonplace',[4] while the *Athenaeum* found it 'not very ingenious, and distinctly dull'.[5] There was a tendency to complain that since Wells had already made one brilliant exploration of the future—in *The Time Machine*—this second attempt to do so, which looked only two centuries ahead, instead of several hundred thousand years, was inevitably anti-climactic.

The truth was that *When the Sleeper Wakes* was not an essay in pure imagination as *The Time Machine* and *The War of the Worlds* had been. It had a perceptible didactic and speculative element, and though the narrative retained some of Wells's earlier vigour, the novel was as much an attempt at systematic prophecy as a work of fiction. As the *Academy* reviewer remarked, in a long critical notice of the book, 'The mistake he has made, we think, is not in prophesying, but in combining a story with his forecasts, and in labelling the result fiction.'[6] This was a perceptive comment, and Wells himself evidently felt the attempted combination to be unsatisfactory, for two years later he completely separated what he called 'the prophetic habit' from the need to tell a story, and produced a collection of speculative essays, *Anticipations*. He subsequently wrote, 'Originally I intended *Anticipations* to be my sole digression from my art or trade (or what you will) of an imaginative writer.'[7] But he was also to regard *Anticipations* as the foundation for all his later intellectual activity, as his remarks to an interviewer in 1906 make clear:

Under the guise of a review of the possibilities of the present

Mr Wells has, in 'Anticipations', made an inventory of the contents of his own mind. In this way he obtained a consistent system of thinking about several important questions. That book, 'Anticipations', is really his thirty-nine articles of creed, his confession of faith, his standpoint. Not having had any other standard of opinion before, his earlier works were often quite simply the result of falling in love with an effect in writing for its own sake.[8]

Between 1899 and 1901 the split between the artist and the prophet or publicist became overt; from the point of view of the latter, the imaginative achievement of his first few years could be dismissed as 'the result of falling in love with an effect in writing for its own sake'. The unhappy mixture of fiction and prophecy in *When the Sleeper Wakes* was the first clear indication that Wells was ceasing to be primarily an artist, responding in imaginative and mythical terms to the life of his times, and was turning to a more directly intellectual treatment of the problems of the present and the possibilities of the future.

As the *Academy* reviewer went on to remind his readers, the attempt to combine fiction and social prophecy was not a new thing; there had been some notable examples in the past few years:

Because *When the Sleeper Wakes* thus becomes neither one thing nor the other: the reader who naturally expects another *War of the Worlds* will be disappointed, the reader who expects another *Looking Backward* will be disappointed; there is here neither the interest of the one nor the social fervour of the other.[9]

Edward Bellamy's *Looking Backward* and William Morris's reply to it, *News from Nowhere*, had appeared in 1888 and 1891 respectively. These two books had described socialist utopias of a very different kind, and both had been widely read and discussed. Despite the differences between them, and the immense literary superiority of Morris's story, the basic structure of the two books is similar: a representative man of the late nineteenth century is mysteriously transported into the world of a century or two hence. Once there he discovers a totally transformed order of society, and he gradually learns of the events, following his own day, that had brought it about. Admittedly, Bellamy's hero reaches the Boston of 2000 by falling into a deep sleep which lasts more than a century, while Morris's hero finally realizes that his experience in utopia has been all a dream, or at least, 'a vision'. Wells takes over this structure in *When the Sleeper Wakes*, and unashamedly borrows Bellamy's device of having his hero fall into a prolonged trance-like sleep. There is no reason why he should not have used this device, but when one compares it with the ingenious conceptual apparatus of *The Time Machine* one can see that Wells's power of invention was flagging. There is considerable ingenuity in the account of the world into which the Sleeper awakes, but, if the familiar Coleridgian distinction is valid here, one might say that whereas *The Time Machine* or *The War of the Worlds* are works of imagination, *When the Sleeper Wakes* is predominantly a work of fancy. In certain specific respects it was remarkably prophetic; but the proliferation of technological details that have since become commonplace does not compensate for the thinness of the underlying concept. The visual sense, that had previously been dominant in Wells's imaginative writing, is curiously weak, and it is very hard to form a coherent picture of the London of 2100:

Mr Wells is continually making too large a demand upon his readers. We doubt not that he himself visualized everything as he went on, but we completely fail to. The result is chaos.[10]

Although the earlier romances had a definite relation to

the contemporary world, this relation was essentially mythical: the theme of *The Time Machine* concerns the class war, and the possibilities of human evolution, but presents them in terms of a wholly symbolic world; similarly, *The War of the Worlds* imaginatively enacts the secret fears and lack of confidence of late Victorian bourgeois society. But the central weakness of *When the Sleeper Awakes* is that it creates its world by directly projecting certain observable tendencies in contemporary society, without subjecting them to any imaginative transmutation or aesthetic distancing. Wells himself described the process a few years later, though he rejected *When the Sleeper Wakes* more for being unsatisfactory as prophecy than bad as literary art:

One becomes more systematic, one sets to work to trace the great changes of the last century or so, and one produces these in a straight line and according to the rule of three. If the maximum velocity of land travel in 1800 was twelve miles an hour and in 1900 (let us say) sixty miles an hour, then one concludes that in 2000 A.D. it will be three hundred miles an hour. If the population of America in 1800—but I refrain from this second instance. In that fashion one got out a sort of gigantesque caricature of the existing world, everything swollen to vast proportions and massive beyond measure. In my case that phase produced a book 'When the Sleeper Wakes', in which, I am told by competent New Yorkers, that I, starting with London, an unbiassed mind, this rule-of-three method, and my otherwise unaided imagination, produced something more like Chicago than any other place wherein righteous men are likely to be found. That I shall verify in due course, but my present point is merely that to write such a book is to discover how thoroughly wrong is this all too obvious method of enlarging the present.[11]

In fact, by 1901, Wells had abandoned the picture of a future London that he had presented in *When the Sleeper Wakes*.[12]

He had come to realize that the great cities of the future would probably not resemble the dense, roofed-over concentration of human beings that he had depicted in his novel, but were much more likely to spread further and further over the countryside as methods of transport improved. And this is more or less what has come about, as the realities of present-day subtopia show. Nevertheless, it is worth remarking that the type of the great city shown in *When the Sleeper Wakes* has had a considerable influence on the iconography of subsequent science fiction. As a modern example, one might mention Isaac Asimov's *The Caves of Steel*, published in 1954, which describes a roofed-in metropolis that reproduces many of the essential characteristics of Wells's London of 2100.

When the Sleeper Wakes is an incoherent book, not only because of the conflict between fiction and prophecy, or the exhaustion of Wells's imagination, though both these factors are important and must be allowed for, but ultimately because it embodies, without any attempt at resolution, the radical ambiguities of its author's intellectual and imaginative attitudes. I have already remarked on the uncertainty of tone of some of Wells's earliest writings; in such an essay as 'The Man of the Year Million' for instance it is impossible to be sure of his attitude to the sensational future developments he is describing. Again, in the early novels we have a more or less delighted acceptance of everyday life, especially the life of the country districts of the Home Counties; this is apparent in *The Wonderful Visit*, *The Wheels of Chance*, and the opening chapters of *The Invisible Man*. But at the same time, we see in *The War of the Worlds* an equally delighted acceptance of the possible destruction of this way of life by the forces symbolizing the future. During his initial period of creative activity the ambiguity of Wells's dual allegiance both to the past and the future was expressed in imaginative and symbolic terms, which transcended the logical problems involved. But from about 1898 onwards Wells's concern with the future was to be expressed in increasingly intellectual terms and his imagination became increasingly coerced by his intellectual convictions. The most crude and grotesque result of this process can be seen in *The Food of the Gods*, but it is already apparent in *When the Sleeper Wakes*. Although this novel is in one sense in the tradition of the utopias of Bellamy and Morris, it differs from them in one very important respect: both these writers attempted to present an image of the future not only as they thought it would be, but as they hoped it would be. Their utopias, in short, embody their authors' desires: Bellamy's for a world where waste and injustice would have been overcome by advanced technology and rather simple-minded social engineering; Morris's for an aesthetic Golden Age of human fraternity. The world of Wells's novel, however, is repulsive rather than desirable: one cannot imagine the London of 2100 as a spur for socialist endeavours to remake society. So much is implied by Wells himself:

He thought of Bellamy, the hero of whose Socialistic Utopia had so oddly anticipated this actual experience. But here was no Utopia, no Socialistic state. He had already seen enough to realize that the ancient antithesis of luxury, waste and sensuality on the one hand and abject poverty on the other, still prevailed (7).

Wells was merely projecting a possible future state of affairs, without in any way implying that it is desirable; still less is he holding it up as an ideal. One would think, rather, that the society discovered by the Sleeper is being presented as an awful warning to present-day humanity; in which case, one could legitimately interpret Wells's intention as satirical. In actual fact, if one examines particular passages of the novel,

146

one gets the impression that an idealizing and a satirical intention are *both* at work, and in effect neutralizing each other. The tone is often ambiguous, with an ultimately vitiating effect on the literary quality. One finds a convenient example of this in Chapter XX, in which Graham, the Sleeper, pays a visit to one of the public eating-houses that have superseded the traditional practice of taking meals in the privacy of the home:

He noted a slight significant thing; the table, as far as he could see, was and remained delightfully neat, there was nothing to parallel the confusion, the broadcast crumbs, the splashes of viand and condiment, the overturned drink and displaced ornaments, which would have marked the stormy progress of the Victorian meal. The table furniture was very different. There were no ornaments, no flowers, and the table was without a cloth, being made, he learnt, of a solid substance having the texture and appearance of damask. He discerned that this damask substance was patterned with gracefully designed trade advertisements.

In a sort of recess before each diner was a complex apparatus of porcelain and metal. There was one plate of white porcelain, and by means of taps for hot and cold volatile fluids the diner washed this himself between the courses; he also washed his elegant white metal knife and fork and spoon as occasion required.

Soup and the chemical wine that was the common drink were delivered by similar taps, and the remaining covers travelled automatically in tastefully arranged dishes down the table along silver rails. The diner stopped these and helped himself at his discretion. They appeared at a little door at one end of the table, and vanished at the other.

This is an undistinguished piece of writing, but the initial difficulty is to decide whether there is an idealizing tendency here or not. Certainly the opposite of this scene, the messy

Victorian dinner table, is mentioned with distaste, so one may assume that Wells is implying that, in this respect, at least, the world of 2100 shows an advance. Nevertheless, the whole passage reads as though it *ought* to be satirical; there is everything to excite the reader's derision in the description, and nothing to attract him. What, for instance, are we to make of the 'chemical wine' or the 'gracefully designed trade advertisements'? There is a succession of inert epithets vaguely suggestive of approval, but conveying no real meaning: 'delightfully neat', 'gracefully designed', 'elegant', 'tastefully arranged'. One inevitably concludes that if Wells is presenting this scene for our approval, he is doing so with a total lack of imaginative conviction, a suggestion certainly borne out by other passages. Wells, in short, *thinks* that some such method of communal feeding would be socially advantageous, if it could be made attractive enough, but his imagination makes only a token attempt to back up the implication.

There is a similar passage in 'A Story of the Days to Come', which was written at about the same time as *When the Sleeper Wakes* and deals with the same society, though without the revolutionary events that enlivened the Sleeper's stay there. A Mr Mwres (otherwise Morris) is described at breakfast:

It was a very different meal from a Victorian breakfast. The rude masses of bread needing to be carved and smeared over with animal fat before they could be made palatable, the still recognizable fragments of recently killed animals, hideously charred and hacked, the eggs torn ruthlessly from beneath some protesting hen,—such things as these, though they constituted the ordinary fare of Victorian times, would have awakened only horror and disgust in the refined minds of the people of these latter days. Instead were pastes and cakes of agreeable and variegated design, without any suggestion in colour or form of the unfortunate animals from which their substance and juices were derived. They appeared on little dishes sliding out upon a rail from a little box at one side of the table.

There is obviously some degree of irony intended here, indeed, the tone is little short of sarcastic, but it is exceedingly difficult to determine which way the irony is directed. Very probably Wells was trying to contrast the barbarities of the heavy Victorian breakfast with the 'elegant' food of the future, but in fact one is not convinced that the bread and butter and bacon and eggs, despite the deliberately unpleasant way of describing them, would be better exchanged for 'pastes and cakes of agreeable and variegated design'. Here, once more, we see Wells's imagination refusing to answer to the demands of his intellectual assumptions. And there is plenty of evidence from the earlier fiction that Wells had no deep-rooted emotional aversion to Victorian eating habits; quite the contrary. Mr Hoopdriver's meals during his cycling holiday in *The Wheels of Chance* are described with distinct relish; and against the calculated disagreeableness of 'the still recognizable fragments of recently killed animals, hideously charred and hacked', one may set the demand by the famished Time Traveller, on his return from the future: 'Save me some of that mutton. I'm starving for a bit of meat.' There are many other passages in *When the Sleeper Wakes* or 'A Story of the Days to Come', that exhibit a similar ambiguity of tone, but the examples quoted should suggest the growing division between Wells's intellectual convictions and his more fundamental attitudes. In the early romances, which were written before he had any clearly formulated extra-literary convictions, his intellect was subject to his imagination and his emotions; but by the late nineties, when Wells was turning towards utopian sociology, he consciously attempted to reverse the process, and the fatal ambiguity of *When the Sleeper Wakes* is a measure of the failure of his imagination to respond.

Nor is this ambiguity merely a question of uncertainty of tone: it is inherent in the very structure of the narrative. In the beginning of the novel Wells endeavours to follow the heuristic method that he employed more or less successfully in several earlier romances; but the Sleeper does not have time to make a gradual exploration of the future world, for almost as soon as he has been awakened he is involved in the revolution of the people, led by Ostrog, against the Council. The attempt to register simultaneously both the Sleeper's unfolding awareness of a strange society, and the tumultuous violence that is sweeping through it, certainly accounts for the confused effect of the early chapters. After the revolution has succeeded, the novel develops a more clear-cut narrative line, though the quality of the writing is no better. In the second part of the book the revolutionary struggle continues, though now it is between the people, reluctantly led by Graham, and Ostrog, their former leader, who is manifestly intent on oppressing and exploiting them. One's immediate impression is that Wells has returned, in a more direct fashion, to the theme of the class-struggle that he had treated symbolically in *The Time Machine*. In the earlier book our sympathies were with the Traveller in his struggle against the 'proletarian' Morlocks; whereas in *When the Sleeper Wakes* it seems that we are to associate ourselves with Graham and the working-class in their desperate struggle for liberation. One might imagine that Wells had suddenly come to think in orthodox—if still rather romanticized—Marxist terms. Yet in this context, the remarks of a Marxist critic are worth quoting:

[Wells] was born into an especially depressed section of the lower middle class: very early he rejected the outlook of that class, and his swift success as a writer carried him out of it economically on to the fringe of the ruling class. But he never lost one of its most marked peculiarities, the fear of the mass of the workers from which it feels itself separated by so narrow a gulf. This fear takes two forms, fear of slipping down into the 'lower world', and fear of an invasion from that world, an invasion of barbarians levelling all before them.

That fear remained with Wells all his life. He might pity the workers, he might want to brighten their lives, but he could never see them as anything but a destructive force which must be led and controlled and, if necessary, coerced. In that interesting early book *When the Sleeper Wakes*, which has a curious and distorted reflection of the class struggle and in which the idea of revolution is not entirely rejected, the workers are exploited and rebellious, but can only revolt under the leadership of a powerful section of the upper class, and the hero of the book, the Sleeper who wakes to find himself the owner of the earth, fights the battle of the workers in isolation as a champion coming to them from the outside. In none of his other books will they play any serious part whatsoever.[13]

That the fear of slipping down into the 'lower world', first exemplified in the Time Traveller's descent into the underworld of the Morlocks, was very much with Wells is apparent if we turn from *When the Sleeper Wakes* to 'A Story of the Days to Come': in that work the two young lovers, Denton and Elizabeth, are forced by poverty to support themselves by manual labour among the lowest social strata; the horror and indignities they undergo—until being rescued by a convenient legacy—are vividly rendered. Although in the final chapters of *When the Sleeper Wakes* Wells was prepared temporarily to reverse his anti-proletarian bias, and presented his hero as the champion of the workers, the interest, as Morton implies, is centred on the gallant struggles of Graham, the lonely hero, finally perishing in his single-handed aeronautic battle against the transport aeroplanes bringing black troops to put down the rebellion. And even here, it is worth noting, Wells was at some pains to exclude the orthodox Marxist doctrine of the ultimate victory of the proletariat, just as he had excluded it in *The Time Machine*. In his preface to the revised edition of 1910 he remarked that he had eliminated 'certain dishonest and regrettable suggestions that the People beat Ostrog. My Graham dies, as all his kind must die, with no certainty of either victory or defeat.'[14]

In fact, there is every indication elsewhere in the book that the future lies with Ostrog, or at least with what he stands for. Although Wells was prepared, for the purposes of his narrative, to involve his readers emotionally with the final romantic struggle of Graham against the followers of Ostrog, it is demonstrable that Ostrog represents Wells's own developing intellectual convictions. Thus, there is a deep-rooted ambiguity at the very heart of the book. Although 'Boss' Ostrog is a politician and not a scientist, he has certain affinities with Wells's earlier romanticized scientists; in particular, his personal appearance is reminiscent of Moreau's:

He was a powerfully built man, as I have said, with a fine forehead and rather heavy features; but his eyes had an odd drooping of the skin above the lids that often comes with advancing years, and the fall of his heavy mouth at the corners gave him an expression of pugnacious resolution (*The Island of Dr Moreau*, 6).

Graham's first impression was of a very broad forehead, very pale blue eyes deep sunken under white brows, an aquiline nose, and a heavily-lined resolute mouth. The folds of flesh over the eyes, the drooping of the corners of the mouth contradicted the upright bearing, and said the man was old (12).

However, there is nothing romantic about Ostrog; he is the supreme realist, though he thinks of manipulating the social body rather as Moreau had manipulated the animal body.

The Nietzschean attitude to morality that had been touched on with Moreau, Griffin, and the 'Diamond Maker', becomes quite explicit with Ostrog:

The coming of the aristocrat is fatal and assured. The end will be the Over-man—for all the mad protests of humanity. Let them revolt, let them win and kill me and my like. Others will arise—other masters. The end will be the same (19).

It becomes quite clear that Ostrog's views are those of Wells himself—or at least those that Wells was to put forward in his own name a couple of years later—if we compare certain passages from Chapter XIX of *When the Sleeper Wakes* ('Ostrog's Point of View') with others from *Anticipations*:

Ostrog looked at him steadfastly. 'The day of democracy is past,' he said. 'Past for ever. That day began with the bowmen of Crecy, it ended when marching infantry, when common men in masses ceased to win the battles of the world, when costly cannon, great ironclads, and strategic railways became the means of power. Today is the day of wealth. Wealth now is power as it never was power before—it commands earth and sea and sky. All power is for those who can handle wealth ... You must accept facts, and these are facts. The world for the Crowd! The Crowd as Ruler! Even in your days that creed had been tried and condemned. Today it has only one believer—a multiplex, silly one,—the man in the Crowd' (19).

I know of no case for the elective Democratic government of modern States that cannot be knocked to pieces in five minutes. It is manifest that upon countless public issues there is no collective will, and nothing in the mind of the average man except blank indifference; that an electional system simply places power in the hands of the most skilful electioneers; that neither men nor their rights are identically equal, but vary with every individual, and, above all, that the minimum or maximum of general happiness is related only so indirectly to the public control that people will suffer great miseries from their governments unre-sistingly, and on the other hand, change their rulers on account of the most trivial irritations. The case against all the prolusions of ostensible Democracy is indeed so strong that it is impossible to consider the present wide establishment of Democratic in-stitutions as being the outcome of any process of intellectual conviction; it arouses suspicion even whether ostensible Demo-cracy may not be a mere rhetorical garment for essentially dif-ferent facts, and upon that suspicion we will now inquire.[15]

Ostrog continues the tentative social speculations that Wells had introduced into *The War of the Worlds* via the Artillery-man; his contempt for the masses and his stress on the need for an aristocratic élite who will do the real work of govern-ing society, directly anticipate the later development of Wells's thought, as set forth in *A Modern Utopia* and similar books. His attitude to the mass of the workers certainly cor-responds to that which Morton attributed to Wells himself:

And what was their hope? What is their hope? What right have they to hope? They work ill and they want the reward of those who work well. The hope of mankind—what is it? That some day the Over-man may come, that some day the inferior, the weak and the bestial may be subdued or eliminated. Subdued if not eliminated. The world is no place for the bad, the stupid, the enervated. Their duty—it's a fine duty too!—is to die. The death of the failure! That is the path by which the beast rose to man-hood, by which man goes on to higher things (19).

One may compare with this Wells's subsequent account of the 'People of the Abyss' in *Anticipations*:

This second consequence of progress is the appearance of a great number of people without either property or any evident func-tion in the social organism. This new ingredient is most apparent in the towns, it is frequently spoken of as the Urban Poor, but its characteristic traits are to be found also in the rural districts. For the most part its individuals are either criminal, immoral, parasitic in more or less irregular ways upon the more successful classes, or labouring, at something less than a regular bare subsistence wage, in a finally hopeless competition against machinery that is as yet not so cheap as their toil. It is, to borrow a popular phrase, the 'submerged' portion of the social body, a leaderless, aimless multitude of people drifting down towards the abyss. Essentially it consists of people who have failed to 'catch on' to the altered necessities the development of mechanism has brought about, they are people thrown out of employment by machinery, thrown out of employment by the escape of industries along some newly opened line of communication to some remote part of the world, or born under circumstances that give them no opportunity of entering the world of active work. Into this welter of machine-superseded toil there topples the non-adaptable residue of every changing trade; its members marry and are given in marriage, and it is recruited by the spendthrifts, weaklings, and failures of every superior class.[16]

I am not concerned in this study with Wells's ideas as such, considered apart from the specific use he made of them in his fiction. It is merely sufficient to note that by the turn of the century Wells had come to think of the romance as not merely an imaginative structure existing in its own right, but as a vehicle for whatever intellectual questions happened to be concerning him. *When the Sleeper Wakes* is the first novel-length romance in which the process is apparent, and there is no doubt that in literary terms it is a failure: Wells himself described it as 'one of the most ambitious and least satisfactory of my books'.[17] Quite apart from the difficulty of combining fiction and prophecy in the same work, the novel is incoherent because of the lack of accord between Wells's speculative intellectual attitudes and his deepest emotional inclinations. In *When the Sleeper Wakes* this conflict becomes overt for the first time in Wells's writing, and destroys the imaginative coherence of the book.

2

When the Sleeper Wakes had been completed early in 1898, though it was not published in book form until May 1899, having first been serialized in the *Graphic*. Late in 1898 or early in 1899 Wells also completed *Love and Mr Lewisham* (the actual date is not clear, since there are some contradictory indications in the *Experiment in Autobiography*)[18] and throughout most of 1899 and part at least of 1900 he seems to have given his imagination the rest it obviously needed, for he appears to have written no fiction during this period, apart from a few short stories. Much of his intellectual energy, one may assume, was taken up with working out more systematically the prophetic speculations that he had hurriedly outlined in *When the Sleeper Wakes*. Yet by 1900 Wells was once more at work on a scientific romance, *The First Men in the Moon*, which was serialized in the *Strand* during 1901, and published as a book in November of that year. Almost simultaneously *Anticipations* was published, after first appearing as a series of essays in the *Fortnightly Review*. The *Athenaeum* remarked:

Mr Wells is certainly a man of most extraordinary energy to be able, at the same time that he publishes his serious book of 'Anticipations', to dash off a pleasant little *Jeu d'esprit* like 'The First Men in the Moon'.[19]

The *Athenaeum* was here indulging in its habitually patronizing attitude to Wells, for *The First Men in the Moon* is certainly more than just 'a pleasant little *Jeu d'esprit*'. Wells himself was to describe it as 'probably the writer's best "scientific romance"',[20] and without going so far as this, one may readily admit that it is a great advance on *When the Sleeper Wakes*. Wells's imagination had recovered a good deal of its earlier vitality, and since he had diverted his prophetic preoccupations into the non-fictional form of *Anticipations* he was able to concentrate much more single-mindedly on the demands of the narrative. Though even in this novel the 'prophetic' note is not absent: the account of Selenite society given in the final section has sociological implications of a characteristic kind.

The First Men in the Moon does not have the originality of conception of Wells's romances of the period 1894–7, even though it has some of their other qualities. In *The War of the Worlds* Wells had treated the theme of interplanetary travel in a completely new fashion, but in *The First Men in the Moon* he reverted to the relatively conventional type of story in which men travel to the moon: an early example is Lucian's *Icaromenippus*, a quotation from which forms the epigraph to Wells's novel. A few decades previously Jules Verne had exploited the theme in *From the Earth to the Moon* and *Round the Moon*, even though his travellers had not been able to land on the moon. What is original in Wells's story is the concept of 'Cavorite', the gravity-resisting substance which enables Bedford and Cavor to travel to the moon, and Bedford finally to return. It is interesting to record the remarks of Verne on *The First Men in the Moon*, as recorded by an interviewer in 1903:

It was inevitable as Jules Verne remarked, that I should speak to him about Wells. 'Je pensais bien que vous alliez me demander cela,' he said. 'His books were sent to me, and I have read them. It is very curious, and, I will add, very English. But I do not see the possibility of comparison between his work and mine . . . It occurs to me that his stories do not repose on very scientific bases. No, there is no *rapport* between his work and mine. I make use of physics. He invents. I go to the moon in a cannon-ball, discharged from a cannon. Here there is no invention. He goes to Mars [*sic*] in an airship, which he constructs of a metal which does away with the law of gravitation. Ça c'est très joli,'

157

cried Monsieur Verne in an animated way, 'but show me this metal. Let him produce it.' [21]

As Wells himself was subsequently to admit, his own romances, unlike Verne's, were not genuinely concerned with scientific possibilities, despite the rhetorical skill with which he introduces his 'inventions', and 'Cavorite' is a decidedly implausible device. Yet though it employs a more conventional kind of narrative than *The Time Machine*, *The War of the Worlds*, or *The Invisible Man*, *The First Men in the Moon* may reasonably be compared to these novels inasmuch as it is an essay in pure imagination, without, excepting the final section, any overt speculative or didactic elements. But, at the same time, it does not have their mythical qualities; it is, quite unashamedly, a story, which engages and attracts the reader's attention solely by the excellence of the narrative elements. As in *The Time Machine*, a realistic opening section is presented in some detail and then contrasted with the wholly exotic world of the central narrative; similarly, the mundane and even banal characteristics of the two main characters act as a means of placing and slightly distancing their exotic surroundings, as had been the case with the Time Traveller in the world of the Eloi. In *The First Men in the Moon* both the realism and the exoticism are more heavily stressed than had been the case in Wells's first novel. Norman Nicholson has remarked on the solidity with which Romney Marsh is established as the setting for Bedford's meeting with Cavor:[22]

Outside the doors of the few cottages and houses that make up the present village, big birch besoms are stuck to wipe off the worst of the clay, which will give some idea of the texture of the district (1).

Again, the contrasted characters of Bedford and Cavor are developed with a gratuitousness which shows that Wells was becoming increasingly concerned with writing realistic fiction. It is significant that Cavor is presented as a wholly benign figure of the traditional 'comic scientist' type: by 1901 Wells seems to have finally exorcized the 'Franken-stein' archetype that had appeared as Moreau and Griffin.

In the lunar scenes Wells was able to describe a strange and exotic world with the same confidence in his own powers that he had displayed in *The Time Machine*. Indeed, many of these scenes show more exuberance of imagination—par-ticularly visual imagination—than any other passages of Wells's writings. In *The Time Machine* the world of 802701 is vividly realized, but for all the strangeness of detail, the contemporary Southern English landscape is somehow apparent through the great cultivated garden in which the Eloi live. The lunar landscapes are, in one sense, wholly 'artificial': the *kind* of imagination that produced them was that which had previously produced the vision of the dying world in the last part of *The Time Machine*. T. S. Eliot, for instance, has called the description of sunrise on the moon 'quite unforgettable'.[23] Equally memorable is the account of the rapid growth of the lunar vegetation in the sunlight:

One after another all down the sunlit slope these miraculous little brown bodies burst and gaped apart, like seed-pods, like the husks of fruits; opened eager mouths that drank in the heat and light pouring in a cascade from the newly-risen sun.

Every moment more of these seed coats ruptured, and even as they did so the swelling pioneers overflowed their rent distended seed-cases and passed into the second stage of growth. With a steady assurance, a swift deliberation, these amazing seeds thrust a rootlet downward to the earth and a queer bundle-like bud into the air. In a little while the slope was dotted with minute plantlets standing at attention in the blaze of the sun.

They did not stand for long. The bundle-like buds swelled and strained and opened with a jerk, thrusting out a coronet of little sharp tips, spreading a whorl of tiny, spiky, brownish leaves, that lengthened rapidly, lengthened visibly even as we watched. The movement was slower than any animal's, swifter than any plant's I have ever seen before. How can I suggest it to you—the way that growth went on? The leaf tips grew so that they moved onward even while we looked at them. The brown seed-case shrivelled and was absorbed with an equal rapidity. Have you ever on a cold day taken a thermometer into your warm hand and watched the little thread of mercury creep up the tube? These moon-plants grew like that (7).

Norman Nicholson has remarked of this passage:

He is taking a score of botanical memories, combining them, inverting them, varying them, and building them up into a cadenza of shining visual beauty. Moreover, it has more than brilliance and integrity; it has that sense of wonder which I think Wells must have felt when, at the Normal School of Science, he first looked through a microscope.[24]

Yet though *The First Men in the Moon* possesses much of the imaginative quality of *The Time Machine* or *The War of the Worlds*, one must emphasize that it does not have the mythical note of these novels. In describing the imaginary panic in London following the Martian invasion, Wells was making certain implications about the society he lived in; in describing the equally imaginary blossoming of the lunar flowers, he was simply exercising his imagination for its own sake. Considered as a story, however, *The First Men in the Moon* could not be bettered: the heuristic method, centred in Bedford's consciousness, is brilliantly employed, and the interest is heightened since Bedford has to record his relationship with Cavor, and their shared responses to the lunar world, in addition to his own particular perceptions. The pace of the narrative is gradually increased until one reaches the climax at the end of Chapter 18, with Bedford racing back to the sphere as the lunar night falls, almost succumbing to the unbearable cold.

Yet no discussion of *The First Men in the Moon* would be complete without examining in some detail the society of the Selenites, of which an account is given in the final chapters, supposedly taken from the radio messages that Cavor sent back to Earth after he had been left alone in the Moon. Wells is here taking advantage of the great imaginative freedom that the novel gave him in order to project an image of a possible society significantly different from that of *The Time Machine*, and far in advance of anything he had dared to outline in *When the Sleeper Wakes* or *Anticipations*, though embodying certain of their tendencies. In his own encounters with the Selenites, Bedford had noticed that they were insect-like creatures with various sub-human characteristics, but had not been able to form any coherent picture of their way of life or social organization. It was left to Cavor to discover the truth about them. Theirs is a world where differentiation according to social function has been taken to the most extreme limits imaginable, supported by systematic biological conditioning:

'In the moon,' says Cavor, 'every citizen knows his place. He is born to that place, and the elaborate discipline of training and education and surgery he undergoes fits him at last so completely to it that he has neither ideas nor organs for any purpose beyond it.' 'Why should he?' Phi-oo would ask. 'If, for example, a Selenite is destined to be a mathematician, his teachers and trainers set out at once to that end. They check any incipient disposition to other pursuits, they encourage his mathematical bias with a perfect psychological skill. His brain grows, or at least the mathematical faculties of his brain grow, and the rest of him only so much as is necessary to sustain this essential part of him. At last, save for rest and food, his one delight lies in the exercise and display of his faculty, his one interest in its application, his sole society the other specialists in his own line. His brain grows continually larger, at least so far as the portions engaging in mathematics are concerned; they bulge ever larger and seem to suck all life and vigour from the rest of his frame. His limbs shrivel, his heart and digestive organs diminish, his insect face is hidden under its bulging contours. His voice becomes a mere stridulation for the stating of formulae; he seems deaf to all but properly enunciated problems. The faculty of laughter, save for the sudden discovery of some paradox, is lost to him; his deepest emotion is the evolution of a novel computation. And so he attains his end' (23).

The Selenite intellectuals, with their enormously developed heads and rudimentary bodies, have obvious affinities with Wells's early 'Man of the Year Million' and the Martians, though they are much more subtly differentiated versions of the type. The stress on intellectual development reaches its peak in the descriptions of the Grand Lunar, a figure who is no doubt meant to be impressive but seems, rather, grotesque to the point of being comic:

He seemed a small, self-luminous cloud at first, brooding on his sombre throne; his braincase must have measured many yards in diameter . . . At first as I peered into the radiating glow, this quintessential brain looked very much like an opaque, featureless bladder with dim, undulating ghosts of convolutions writhing visibly within. Then beneath its enormity and just above the edge of the throne one saw with a start minute elfin eyes peering out of the glow. No face, but eyes, as if they peered through holes. At first I could see no more than these two staring little eyes, and then below I distinguished the little dwarfed body and its insect-jointed limbs, shrivelled and white. The eyes stared down at me with a strange intensity, and the lower part of the swollen globe was wrinkled. Ineffectual-looking little hand-tentacles steadied this shape on the throne . . . I saw that shadowy attendants were busy spraying that great brain with a cooling spray, and patting and sustaining it (24).

The obsession with brain-capacity as a physical sign of intellectual ability was to remain with Wells throughout his life, as the following quotation from a late work will show:

With a few more cubic inches of brain for the average man and a score of years added to the span of life, or even with such an economy of mental exertion through simplification as would be equivalent to these extensions, every present difficulty in the human outlook would vanish like a dream.[25]

Inevitably the extravagant descriptions of the Selenite world suggest a satirical intention, but the general effect is extremely ambiguous. The kind of uncertainly directed irony apparent in parts of *When the Sleeper Wakes* and 'A Story of the Days to Come' is once more evident:

The making of these various sorts of operative must be a very curious and interesting process. I am still very much in the dark about it, but quite recently I came upon a number of young Selenites, confined in jars from which only the fore-limbs protruded, who were being compressed to become machine-minders of a special sort. The extended 'hand' in this highly developed system of technical education is stimulated by irritants and nourished by injection, while the rest of the body is starved. Phi-oo, unless I misunderstood him, explained that in the earlier stages these queer little creatures are apt to display signs of suffering in their various cramped situations, but they easily become indurated to their lot; and he took me on to where a number of flexible-limbed messengers were being drawn out and broken in. It is quite unreasonable, I know, but such glimpses of the educational methods of these beings affect me disagreeably. I hope, however, that may pass off and I may be able to see more of this aspect of this wonderful social order. That wretched-looking hand-tentacle sticking out of its jar seemed to have a sort of limp appeal for lost possibilities; it haunts me still, although, of course, it is really in the end a far more humane proceeding than our earthly method of leaving children to grow into human beings, and then making machines of them (23).

The ambiguity of Wells's attitude to his Selenite society was remarked on by a reviewer, who referred to

a certain amount of satire, in which the author seems divided between a purpose of showing, by the method of reduction to the absurd, the iniquity of our social system, and an intention of deriding us for that we have not yet carried it out to its furthest consequences.[26]

It would be wrong to suggest that Wells would have unreservedly approved of Selenite society in all its aspects, but it represented an extreme, and even grotesque, type of the totally organized social order that was increasingly to be the ideal of his utopian speculations. Since the Selenites are drawn with the same imaginative exuberance that characterizes the rest of the novel, we are not conscious of any transition from pure narrative to sociological speculation, and the very grotesqueness of this insect-like race prevents too immediate comparisons between them and recognizable humanity. Yet there can be no doubt that Wells's picture of Selenite society embodies the characteristic ambiguities of his thinking at this period. Like Mr Cavor, confronting the young Selenites confined in jars to become machine minders, he both admires a society that could do such things, and is dismayed by the results in practice.

Within the limits that I have indicated, *The First Men in the Moon* is a successful work, and an unquestionably entertaining one. It can be seen as the final flowering of Wells's initial phase of intense imaginative activity, and so is a suitable work with which to conclude this study.

CHAPTER VII

WELLS AND THE TWENTIETH CENTURY

At the time of his death, Wells had published over a hundred books; the majority could be classed as fiction, but there was also a large amount of discursive writing on every conceivable subject. The emphasis of the present study has fallen on the imaginative works that Wells wrote before 1901, and some readers may consider that this concentration on such a brief period at the beginning of his career is somewhat disproportionate. But as I stated in my opening chapter, I am assuming as axiomatic that the bulk of Wells's published output has lost whatever *literary* interest it might have had, and is not likely to regain it in the foreseeable future, whatever value it may possess for the social historian or the historian of ideas. As F. R. Leavis has remarked, apropos of Wells, 'there is an elementary distinction to be made between the *discussion* of problems and ideas, and what we find in the great novelists'.[1] There is no doubt that Wells did come to conceive of the novel as in large measure a medium for 'the discussion of problems and ideas'. In 1911 he wrote of the modern novel, 'it is the only medium through which we can discuss the great majority of the problems which are being raised in such bristling multitude by our contemporary social development'.[2] The inevitable result of this misconceived attitude to the craft of fiction is that the novels in question lose their validity and interest as soon as the ideas and problems discussed in them cease to be live contemporary issues. And this has been the fate of almost all Wells's fiction written since 1901, apart from a handful of comedies. It was precisely my sense of the deadness of most of Wells's fictional *oeuvre* that led me to concentrate my attention on that part of it which seemed most alive, namely, the romances that he wrote during the opening years of his literary career. I hope that the preceding chapters will have justified the attempt.

The picture that will have emerged from them, of the young Wells as a symbolic and mythopoeic writer whose work has closer affinities to poetry than to the conventional realistic fiction of his time, will no doubt seem strange and even incredible to those who are more familiar with his later career. Yet there need be nothing inherently surprising in the discovery that Wells's romances offer a multiplicity of meanings, of most of which, we may assume, he was unaware. It is part of Wells's achievement in these works that he wrote about a good deal more than he intended. As G. K. Chesterton observed, a long time before the doctrine of the 'intentional fallacy' was formulated:

Either criticism is no good at all (a very defensible position) or else criticism means saying about an author the very things that would have made him jump out of his boots.[3]

It is quite possible that Wells intended his early romances to be no more than works of light entertainment, without deeper implications, but that is no reason why the modern reader should be content to regard them as such.

It is true, of course, that Wells had received a scientific education, and that his later attitudes were severely positivistic. Yet, as we have seen, he had been absorbing fictional romance from childhood, long before he embarked on his studies at South Kensington. And much as he admired his teacher, Thomas Huxley, his earliest surviving picture of a man of science, Dr Nebogipfel in *The Chronic Argonauts*, owes much more to Frankenstein and the ancient tradition of the mage and the alchemist. And we may safely assume that there was a fairly close degree of identification between the idealized figure of Nebogipfel and the young Wells. Both of them were 'born out of their time', and Nebogipfel's aspirations towards the future, as well as being a common *fin de siècle* motif, represented an ideal that was to remain constant with Wells throughout most of his life, though expressed in a great variety of forms.

Nebogipfel's immediate descendant, the Time Traveller, is a conventional bourgeois rather than a Frankenstein type, and he does not have Nebogipfel's urge to escape to his rightful heritage in the future. In fact, he seems to use his invention for nothing more than glorified joy-riding. Yet neither does he regard science as a means of pursuing truth for its own sake, nor as a way of benefiting the human community at large. His attitude to research is purely personal, and like Nebogipfel, his main concern is to escape from the immediate confines of his temporal situation. Both Moreau and Griffin are further versions of the Frankenstein type (though Griffin perhaps owes more to Stevenson's Dr Jekyll, and Moreau is also a perverted Prospero figure), and they both regard their scientific attainments as a means of increasing their personal power. Neither of them would dream of publishing their discoveries in the normal fashion, and Griffin is at great pains to keep his discovery of invisibility from the Professor at the provincial college where he works. The use they make of their powers is far from being beneficent, and both undergo an ultimate self-immolation (Nebogipfel and the Time Traveller before them had been permanently cast out of the world to an unknown fate). As I have suggested, there is an almost ritualistic air about the final hunting down and killing of the Invisible Man, suggesting that Wells was ridding himself of the Frankenstein type, the scientist as romantic individualist, and all that he could be imagined as standing for.

Certainly, in so far as Wells can be thought of as identifying himself even partially with these figures, he was aligned with an 'alchemical' view of science that was very different from anything he could have absorbed in the sober atmosphere of the Royal College of Science. It is important to realize that they were emotional and imaginative projections, and had nothing to do with his intellectual convictions. Indeed, despite his speculative interest in Marx and Darwin, Wells seems to have had virtually no firm intellectual convictions of any kind during the early and mid-nineties. His scepticism about the beneficent possibilities of science had been manifested in 1891 in the final paragraph of his essay, 'The Rediscovery of the Unique', and his sceptical attitude to most forms of human enterprise is evident in the generalized satire of *The Wonderful Visit.* I would, in fact, go so far as to claim that it was this intellectual scepticism that allowed his imagination free play, and so led to the literary achievement of his early romances. One thinks of Keats's celebrated remark about the quality necessary 'to form a Man of Achievement, especially in Literature . . . *Negative Capability*, that is, when a man is capable of being in uncertainties, mysteries, doubts, without any irritable reaching after fact and reason . . .' This, I think, is peculiarly applicable to Wells during the formative years 1894–7, when his imagination was, in all essentials, functioning poetically. In a letter written to Arnold Bennett in 1900, Wells remarked of his romances:

But that other stuff which you would have me doing day by day is no more to be done day by day than repartees or lyric poetry. The Imagination moves in a mysterious way its wonders to perform. I can assure you that I am *not* doing anything long and weird and strong in the vein of *The Time Machine* and I never intend to. I would as soon take hat and stick and start out into the street to begin a passionate love. If it comes—well and good.[4]

Yet it was not to be expected that a writer of Wells's powerful if undisciplined intellectual powers would remain for long without some 'irritable reaching after fact and reason'. By the late nineties he was becoming increasingly interested in sociology, and the Fabian Society was soon to exercise a crucial influence on his intellectual development. As he wrote in his autobiography:

Here I am not dealing so much with these ideological limitations with which I presently fell foul, as with their pervading sense of the importance of social service as their frame of life, and the way in which Jane and I were probably influenced by them. We may have had that in us from the beginning, Jane particularly, but they have brought it out in us. They may have done much to deflect me from the drift towards a successful, merely literary career into which I was manifestly falling in those early Sandgate days. I might have become an artist and a literary careerist and possibly a distinguished one, and then my old friend Osborn of the *National Observer*, the *Morning Post* and 'Boon' would never have had occasion to call my books 'sociological cocktails'.[5]

The shift from a dominantly individualistic view of human life to a collectivist one was made with great rapidity once Wells had started to absorb these influences, which provided him with a set of intellectual convictions on which all his later speculative activity was to be based. It is one of Wells's more disconcerting attributes that he could undergo in a few months the kind of change in intellectual stance that would take another man as many years. As Chesterton was to remark:

I have always thought that he reacted too swiftly to everything; possibly as a part of the swiftness of his natural genius. I have never ceased to admire and sympathize; but I think he has always been too much in a state of reaction.[6]

But although Wells's thought quickly accepted a collectivist frame of reference, he did not abandon his earlier and fundamental individualism. The inevitable product of the combination of these two attitudes was the doctrine of the 'élite', the governing aristocracy of technologists and managers, that was to remain basic in all Wells's social thinking. It is first hinted at as early as 1897, in the Artilleryman's speculations in *The War of the Worlds* about the kind of resistance movement that must be started to survive the Martian occupation. In April 1899 we find Wells telling an interviewer, 'What seems to be inevitable in the future is rule by an aristocracy of organizers, men who manage railroads and similar vast enterprises',[7] and the same idea is put forward, in more extravagant terms, in Ostrog's remarks about the inevitability of an aristocracy in *When the Sleeper Wakes*. The doctrine of the managerial élite is stated at length in *Anticipations*, and it reappears in the guise of the Samurai of *A Modern Utopia*, the Open Conspirators of various of Wells's writings in the twenties, and the Airmen of *The Shape of Things to Come* (1933).

Similarly, the 'alchemical' attitude to science that we associate with Moreau or Griffin was changed when it was brought into line with Wells's newly acquired intellectual collectivism, but by no means totally transformed. Science is to be used for the good of humanity at large, rather than the self-aggrandizement of the scientific individualist, and the élite who are to control its use are credited with automatically possessing the moral wisdom so conspicuously lacked by a Griffin or a Moreau. Yet the belief in its quasi-magical powers totally to transform the human environment and the very nature of life itself, is taken over from the early romances and amplified in the process. This is apparent in *The Food of the Gods*, where the discovery of Herakleophorbia leads ultimately to the race of giants with whom, it is assumed, the future of humanity is to lie. The combination of almost limitless scientific possibilities with large-scale social engineering was to produce the characteristic 'Wellsian' utopia, adumbrated first in *A Modern Utopia* in 1905, and subsequently revised from time to time (and brilliantly satirized in E. M. Forster's short story 'The Machine Stops'). Perhaps its most elaborate exposition is to be found in *The Shape of Things to Come*, a work which contains flashes of genuine imaginative invention, but is largely vitiated by the banality and naivety of its underlying conception.

There is no need to labour the point which I have already put forward: that Wells's acceptance of a collectivist ideology and the Fabian ideal of 'social service' destroyed the autonomy of his imagination, and radically reduced his stature as a literary artist. From *The Food of the Gods* onward his imagination, still extremely fertile in many respects, was dragooned into the didactic service of his sociological ideas. Anthony West has suggested, very plausibly, that Wells never wholly acquiesced in this process, and that there was always a certain tension between Wells's progressivism and the remains of his original scepticism (and its accompanying pessimism):

Wells' 'progressive' writing represents an attempt to straddle irreconcilable positions, and it involved a perpetual conflict of a wasteful character. In all too much of his work he is engaged in shouting down his own better judgment.[8]

Yet although Wells ceased to be an artist in his longer scientific romances after the publication of *The First Men in the Moon* in 1901, the vein of realistic comedy that had begun with *The Wheels of Chance* in 1896 was to continue unchecked for another ten years. In *Kipps* and *The History of Mr Polly*, at least, Wells's imagination was still free to exploit and re-create his own earliest experience in a memorable form. Wells subsequently claimed that even these works had a specific didactic purpose, by showing Kipps and Polly as victims of society, whose tribulations were due to their lack of education. He no doubt needed to make such a claim, to guard against the self-accusation of writing simply for the sake of writing, but the pleasure that innumerable readers have got from these books has nothing at all to do with any didactic purpose. Wells could not go on drawing indefinitely on the material of his own early life, though he was still able to exploit it successfully as late as *Bealby* (1915). His later realistic fiction, which is much given to the 'discussion of ideas and problems', is self-imitative, and parasitic in a very discernible way on his Edwardian work. Thus, *Christina Alberta's Father* (1925) draws on *Ann Veronica* (not itself a work that has stood up very well to the passing of time), while the very late *You Can't be Too Careful* (1941) is a somewhat soured attempt to re-use the substance of *Kipps* and *Mr Polly*.

Wells is remembered and admired as the author of *Kipps* and *Mr Polly*, and, perhaps, *Tono-Bungay*. But these works apart, the popular image of Wells is still largely that of the tireless planner of a utopian world. Anthony West quotes some remarks by Dr J. Bronowski that support this view:

H. G. Wells used to write stories in which tall, elegant engineers administered with perfect justice a society in which other people had nothing to do but be happy: the Houyhnhnms administering the Yahoos. Wells used to think this a very fine world; but it was only 1984. . . .[9]

The history of the world in the last thirty years had done

nothing to support Wells's faith in human perfectibility, and a good deal to undermine it. That he himself came to realize this is evident from the despairing incoherence of *Mind at the End of its Tether*, published the year before he died. Yet the hollowness and inadequacy of Wells's utopian aspirations are readily apparent, even if we do not see them in the light of subsequent world events. Wells had a temperamental strain of impatience that made him incapable of tolerating the difficulties and problems and disappointments that are inextricably part of the texture of normal life. He wished, in short, for a world where nothing would ever go wrong; or, in other words, a world where no one need ever grow up. He had, in fact, ignored the warning of his old teacher, Thomas Huxley, who, whilst hoping that the evil of the world may be abated, had added the warning, 'I deem it an essential condition of the realization of that hope that we should cast aside the notion that the escape from pain and sorrow is the proper object of life.' [10] For all their elaborate apparatus of applied science and social engineering, Wells's utopias are the projection of a radically immature view of human existence. Perhaps the best possible comment on them was that made by Chesterton as long ago as 1905.

And the weakness of all Utopias is this, that they take the greatest difficulty of man and assume it to be overcome, and then give an elaborate account of the overcoming of the smaller ones. They first assume that no man will want more than his share, and then are very ingenious in explaining whether his share will be delivered by motor-car or balloon. [11]

Nevertheless, if my contention is correct, the works that Wells produced during those early years when he was writing as an artist, and not as a propagandist, should ensure that his reputation lives among those who are interested primarily in literature, however absorbing the historians of society or ideas may find the rest of his work. Few young men have written so much that was new and wonderful in so short a time.

SELECT BIBLIOGRAPHY

(Unless otherwise stated, the place of publication is London)

BOOKS BY H. G. WELLS

The Time Machine: An Invention, 1895
Select Conversations with an Uncle, 1895
The Wonderful Visit, 1895
The Stolen Bacillus and Other Incidents, 1895
The Island of Dr Moreau, 1896
The Plattner Story and Others, 1897
The Invisible Man: A Grotesque Romance, 1897
*Certain Personal Matters: A Collection of Material, Mainly Auto-
    biographical*, 1898 [1897]
The War of the Worlds, 1898
When the Sleeper Wakes, 1899 (Reissued in 1910 as *The Sleeper
    Awakes*)
Tales of Space and Time, 1900 [1899]
The First Men in the Moon, 1901
Anticipations, 1902 [1901]
Twelve Stories and a Dream, 1903
The Food of the Gods and How it Came to Earth, 1904
A Modern Utopia, 1905
The Country of the Blind, 1911
The Short Stories of H. G. Wells, 1927
The Scientific Romances of H. G. Wells, 1933
Experiment in Autobiography (2 vols.), 1934

UNCOLLECTED ITEMS BY H. G. WELLS

(The titles recorded here only represent a small proportion of
    Wells's journalistic output during the years 1893–7)

'A Tale of the Twentieth Century' (by 'S. B.'), *Science Schools
    Journal*, May 1887

175

The Chronic Argonauts, *Science Schools Journal*, April, May, June 1888

'The Rediscovery of the Unique', *Fortnightly Review*, lvi (1891)

★ 'The Literature of the Future', *Pall Mall Gazette*, 11 October 1893

★ 'The Man of the Year Million', *Pall Mall Budget*, 16 November 1893 (reprinted in *Certain Personal Matters* as 'Of a Book Unwritten')

★ 'Angels, Plain and Coloured', *Pall Mall Gazette*, 5 December 1893

★ 'Time Travelling. Possibility or Paradox?', *National Observer*, 17 March 1894

★ 'The Time Machine', ibid., 24 March 1894

★ 'A.D. 12,203. A Glimpse of the Future', ibid., 31 March 1894

★ 'The Refinement of Humanity. A.D. 12,203', ibid., 21 April 1894

★ 'The Sunset of Mankind', ibid., 28 April 1894

★ 'In the Underworld', ibid., 19 May 1894

★ 'The Time-Traveller Returns', ibid., 23 June 1894

★ 'The Limits of Individual Plasticity', *Saturday Review*, 19 January 1895

★ 'Intelligence on Mars', ibid., 4 April 1896

'The Novels of Mr George Gissing', *Contemporary Review*, lxxii (1897)

'The Romance of the Scientist' (interview), *The Young Man*, August 1897

'Realism v. Romance' (interview), *To-day*, 11 September 1897

'What I Believe' (interview), *The Puritan*, i (1899)

'H. G. Wells, Esq., B.Sc.', *Royal College of Science Magazine*, xv (April 1903)

'H. G. Wells' (interview), *New York Herald*, 15 April 1906

'An Experiment in Illustration' (introducing a condensed and newly illustrated version of *The War of the Worlds*), *Strand Magazine*, lix (February 1920)

★ Unsigned.

SELECT BIBLIOGRAPHY

OTHER MATERIAL

OTHER MATERIAL

AMIS, KINGSLEY, *New Maps of Hell: A Survey of Science Fiction*, 1961

BELGION, MONTGOMERY, *H. G. Wells*, 1953

BERESFORD, J. D., *H. G. Wells*, 1915

BERGONZI, BERNARD, 'Another Early Wells Item', *Nineteenth Century Fiction*, xiii (1958)

—— 'The Publication of *The Time Machine* 1894–5', *Review of English Studies*, n.s. xi (1960)

—— '*The Time Machine*: An Ironic Myth', *Critical Quarterly*, ii (1960)

BROME, VINCENT, *H. G. Wells*, 1951

BROOKS, VAN WYCK, *The World of H. G. Wells*, New York, 1915

CAUDWELL, CHRISTOPHER, 'H. G. Wells: A Study in Utopianism', *Studies in a Dying Culture*, 1938

CHESTERTON, G. K., 'Mr H. G. Wells and the Giants', *Heretics*, 1905

CONNES, G. A., 'La première forme de la Machine à explorer le temps', *Revue Anglo-Americaine*, i (1924)

—— *Etude sur la Pensée de Wells*, Paris, 1926

EDEL, LEON and GORDON N. RAY (eds.), *Henry James and H. G. Wells*, 1958

GERBER, RICHARD, *Utopian Fantasy*, 1955

HAIGHT, GORDON S., 'H. G. Wells's "The Man of the Year Million"', *Nineteenth Century Fiction*, xii (1958)

MOORE, PATRICK, *Science and Fiction*, 1957

MORTON, A. L., *The English Utopia*, 1952

NICHOLSON, NORMAN, *H. G. Wells*, 1950

PRITCHETT, V. S., 'The Scientific Romances', *The Living Novel*, 1946

RAY, GORDON N., 'H. G. Wells Tries to be a Novelist', *Edwardians and Late Victorians* (English Institute Essays 1959), New York, 1960

RICHARDS, GRANT, *Memories of a Misspent Youth*, 1932

SHANKS, EDWARD, 'The Work of Mr H. G. Wells', *First Essays on Literature*, 1923

SHERARD, ROBERT H., 'Jules Verne Revisited', *T.P.'s Weekly*, 9 October 1903

WEEKS, ROBERT P., 'Disentanglement as a Theme in H. G. Wells's Fiction', *Papers of the Michigan Academy of Science, Arts and Letters*, xxxix (1954)

WELLS, GEOFFREY H., *The Works of H. G. Wells: A Bibliography, Dictionary and Subject Index*, 1926

—— *H. G. Wells: A Sketch for a Portrait* (published under the pseudonym of 'Geoffrey West'), 1930

WEST, ANTHONY, 'H. G. Wells', *Principles and Persuasions*, 1958

WILSON, HARRIS (ed.), *Arnold Bennett and H. G. Wells*, 1960

APPENDIX

Two Stories by H. G. Wells
reprinted from
The Science Schools Journal
1887–8

A TALE OF THE TWENTIETH CENTURY

For Advanced Thinkers

CHAPTER I

Years had passed. . . .

The Inventor had died in a garret. Too proud to receive parish relief, he had eaten every article of clothing he possessed, scraped off and assimilated every scrap of the plaster on the walls of his wretched apartment, gnawed his finger nails down to the quick, and—died.

His body was found a mere mass of bones, a result of the disproportionate amount of lime in his too restricted dietary.

But though the Inventor was dead, the Thought was not.

That commercial enterprise to which this nation owes its greatness, its position in the vanguard of the armies of progress, had taken the thing up. The pawnbroker, to whom the Inventor had pledged his patent rights for thirteen shillings and sixpence, this pawnbroker, Isaac Meluish, type of sustaining capital, organized a Youarenowgoingtobetoldwhatsodontgoagettingimpatient Company Limited, and made it a practical thing.

The idea was this—

A locomotive of a new type. The wheels rotated by electricity, generated by a dynamo-electric machine, worked by the rotation of the wheels. It will be obvious, that all that is required in such a machine is an initial velocity, to ensure an exceedingly efficient and durable motive force. This initial velocity was furnished by the agency of compressed air.

This idea Isaac Meluish developed: he took the underground railway, the idea, numerous influential persons, and a prospectus, and mixed them up judiciously, so that the influential persons became identified with the prospectus. Scrip was then issued, and the whole conception crystallized out as a definite tangible thing.

The 'Metropolitan and District' was to undergo a second birth from the Meluish brain. No longer were AS_2O_3 and SO_2 to undermine the health of London. Ozone was to abound exceedingly. Invalids were no longer to repair to and at the seaside: they could train on the Underground.

The tunnels were to be illuminated and decorated.

Moreover, the shares of the companies connected with the enterprise were to go up to infinity and stay there—like Elijah.

August persons took shares, and in part paid for them.

It was resolved to make the adoption of the new idea a Britannic festival. A representative cargo of passengers was to travel in the first train round the Inner Circle. The sole lessee and actor of the Lyceum Theatre was to perform all at once every one of the parts he had ever previously taken, admission gratis. There was to be a banquet to the British great ones at the Crystal Palace, and an unsectarian national thanksgiving at the Albert Hall.

July 19th, 1999, approached.

All was lissomness of heart.

*   *   *

It was July 19th, 1999. The nave of the Crystal Palace was brilliantly lit and gorgeously adorned. All the able, all the eloquent, all the successful, all the prosperous, were banqueting below. In the galleries, clustered unnumbered mediocrity: innumerable half guineas had been paid to secure the privilege of watching those great men eat. There were 19

Bishops in evening dress, 4 Princes and their interpreters, 12 Dukes, A Strong Minded Female, the P.R.A., 14 popular professors, 1 learned ditto, 70 Deans (assorted), the President of the Materialistic Religious Society, a popular low comedian, 1,604 eminent wholesale and retail drapers, hatters, grocers, and tea dealers, a reformed working man M.P., and honorary directors of well nigh the universe, 203 stockbrokers, 1 Earl (in a prominent place), who had once said a remarkably smart thing, 9 purely Piccadilly Earls, 13 sporting Earls, 17 trading ditto, 113 bankers, a forger, 1 doctor, 12 theatrical managers, Bludsole the mammoth novelist, 1 electrician (from Paris), a multitude no man could number of electrical company directors, their sons and their sons' sons, their cousins, their nephews, their uncles, their parents, and their friends, the leading legal stars, 2 advertisement contractors, 41 patent medicine manufacturers, 'Lords, Senators, a Spirit Raiser, a Soothsayer, foreign Musicians, Officers, Captains, Guards, &c.'

A great man was speaking.

The people in the galleries could hear—'*twang*, twang, TWANG, *twang*, twang'. Those around the great man heard 'little know whirrrrr erprise—daring energies of the race— (*great applause*)—wherrererer ergree with me in this marr that (*sssh!*)—scale inaccessible mountains, nay—MORE. Bore them through, nullify them—(TREMENDOUS APPLAUSE)— murr rr rrr rrr—(*loud and prolonged cheering*)—burr, burr, burr—(FRANTIC APPLAUSE. *Sssh!*)—daring yet calculating; bold yet rr, burr, burr, burr——'

Thus was the great man speaking apparently, when a telegram was handed to *Sir* Isaac Meluish. He glanced at it, and turning a pale lavender colour, sunk beneath the table.

          ★   ★   ★

Let us leave him there.

Chapter II

This had happened. The representative passengers had assembled. There were an August Person, his keeper, the Premier, two Bishops, several popular actresses, four generals (home department), various exotics, a person apparently connected with the navy, the Education Minister, 124 public service parasites, an idiot, the President of the Board of Trade, a suit of clothes, bankers, another idiot, shopkeepers, forgers, scene painters, still another idiot, directors, &c. (as per previous sample). The representative passengers had entrained. By means of the compressed air, a high velocity had been attained. The scientific manager had smilingly remarked to the august person, 'We will, an' it please you, first run round the Inner Circle and see the decorations.' All had gone as merry as a muffin bell.

Never had the conscientious desire of the august person to take an interest in everything been more conspicuous. He *insisted*—really *insisted*—on the scientific manager taking him on to the motor, and explaining it in detail.

'All that I have been showing you,' said the scientific manager (a small and voluble mechanism), concluding the display, 'is of English manufacture. You know the great firm of Schulz and Brown of Pekin (they removed there in 1920 in order to obtain cheap labour)—and it is consequently sound and strong in every particular. I must now explain the stopping action. I may mention here that the original inventor designed an engine carrying a considerable store of compressed air. *I* have improved on this. The rotary action not only works the dynamo, but also compresses air for the next start. Actually there is *no* force put into this thing from without, from this moment until it breaks, it costs us *nothing* in working. Talking of breaks, I must now show you them.' And the scientific manager, smiling with the approving consciousness of a joke, looked round him. Apparently he did not see what he wanted, his searching eye became more eager. He flushed somewhat. 'Baddelay,' said he, 'how are the brakes worked?'

'I *dun*' no,' said Baddelay; 'these here 'andils, wot *I* took for brakes broke orf, bein' touched; bein', apparently, plaster o' Paris deckerashuns.'

Thereupon the hues of the scientific manager's face hurried through the spectrum at a tremendous rate, from strontium red to thallium green. And he said to the august personage, 'The breaks are broke'; and he added, his voice assuming the while, that low, clear tone only heard from men struggling against overwhelming emotion, 'Look at that manometer.'

'I think,' said the august person, 'I won't see anything else, thank you; I would prefer not. I should like to get out now if you can manage it. The high velocity is unpleasant.'

'Sire,' said the scientific manager, 'we *can not* stop. And, moreover, that manometer warns me that before us is a choice of two things: to double our speed or to be blown to fragments by the ever-increasing tension of the compressed air.'

'In this sudden and unexpected emergency,' said the great one, with a vague recollection of Parliamentary first nights, 'it is perhaps advisable to increase the speed as suddenly as possible.'

*   *   *

The Crystal Palace meeting broke up in confusion, and the banquet became a battle for hats. Boanerges at the Albert Hall, uttering unsectarian platitudes on the heaven-sent prosperity of this land, received a telegram and preached thereafter on the text, 'Vanitas vanitatum'. The dismay slowly spreading from these foci, flashed over the entire land with the evening papers.

Chapter III

What was to be done?

What *could* be done?

The matter might have been raised in the Senate, had not the unexpected absence of the Speaker (he was in the train) prevented the meeting of the governing body. A popular meeting in Trafalgar Square to consider the matter was automatically suppressed by a new method.

Meanwhile the fated train whirled round the circle with ever-increasing velocity. Early on the 20th the end came.

Between Victoria and Sloane Square the train left the lines, dashing violently through the walls of the track and throttling itself among a subterranean network of water-pipes, gaspipes, and drains. There was an awful pause, broken only by the falling in of the houses on either side of the scene of the catastrophe. Then a terrific explosion rent the air.

Most of the passengers were utterly destroyed. The august person, however, came down all right in Germany. The commercial speculators descended in foreign regions in the form of blight.

Published over the initials 'S.B.'
in *The Science Schools Journal*, May 1887.

THE CHRONIC ARGONAUTS

PART I

THE STORY FROM AN EXOTERIC POINT OF VIEW

Being the Account of Dr Nebogipfel's sojourn in Llyddwdd

About half-a-mile outside the village of Llyddwdd by the road that goes up over the eastern flank of the mountain called Pen-y-pwll to Rwstog is a large farm-building known as the Manse. It derives this title from the fact that it was at one time the residence of the minister of the Calvinistic Methodists. It is a quaint, low, irregular erection, lying back some hundred yards from the roadway, and now fast passing into a ruinous state.

Since its construction in the latter half of the last century this house has undergone many changes of fortune, having been abandoned long since by the farmer of the surrounding acres for less pretentious and more commodious head-quarters. Among others Miss Carnot, 'the Gallic Sappho' at one time made it her home, and later on an old man named Williams became its occupier. The foul murder of this tenant by his two sons was the cause of its remaining for some considerable period uninhabited; with the inevitable consequence of its undergoing very extensive dilapidation.

The house had got a bad name, and adolescent man and Nature combined to bring swift desolation upon it. The fear of the Williamses which kept the Llyddwdd lads from gratifying their propensity to invade its deserted interior, manifested itself in unusually destructive resentment against its external breakables. The missiles with which they at once confessed and defied their spiritual dread, left scarcely a splinter of glass, and only battered relics of the old-fashioned leaden frames, in its narrow windows; while numberless shattered tiles about the house, and four or five black apertures yawning behind naked rafters in the roof, also witnessed vividly to the energy of their trajection. Rain and wind thus had free way to enter the empty rooms and work their will there, old Time aiding and abetting. Alternately soaked and desiccated, the planks of flooring and wainscot warped apart strangely, split here and there, and tore themselves away in paroxysms of rheumatic pain from the rust-devoured nails that had once held them firm. The plaster of walls and ceiling, growing green-black with a rain-fed crust of lowly life, parted slowly from the fermenting laths; and large fragments thereof falling down inexplicably in tranquil hours, with loud concussion and clatter, gave strength to the popular superstition that old Williams and his sons were fated to re-enact their fearful tragedy until the final judgment. White roses and daedal creepers, that Miss Carnot had first adorned the walls with, spread now luxuriantly over the lichen-filmed tiles of the roof, and in slender graceful sprays timidly invaded the ghostly cobweb-draped apartments. Fungi, sickly pale, began to displace and uplift the bricks in the cellar floor; while on the rotting wood everywhere they clustered, in all the glory of purple and mottled crimson, yellow-brown and hepatite. Wood-lice and ants, beetles and moths, winged and creeping things innumerable, found each day a more congenial home among the ruins; and after them in ever-increasing multitudes swarmed the blotchy toads. Swallows and martins built every year more thickly in the silent, airy, upper chambers. Bats and owls struggled for the crepuscular corners of the lower rooms. Thus, in the Spring of the year eighteen hundred and eighty-seven, was Nature taking over, gradually but certainly, the tenancy of the old Manse. 'The house was falling into decay,' as men who do not appreciate the application of human derelicts to other beings' use would say, 'surely and swiftly.' But it was destined nevertheless to shelter another human tenant before its final dissolution.

There was no intelligence of the advent of a new inhabitant in quiet Llyddwdd. He came without a solitary premonition out of the vast unknown into the sphere of minute village observation and gossip. He fell into the Llyddwdd world, as it were, like a thunderbolt falling in the daytime. Suddenly, and out of nothingness, he *was*. Rumour, indeed, vaguely averred that he was seen to arrive by a certain train from London, and to walk straight without hesitation to the old Manse, giving neither explanatory word nor sign to mortal as to his purpose there: but then the same fertile source of information also hinted that he was first beheld skimming down the slopes of steep Pen-y-pwll with exceeding swiftness, riding, as it appeared to the intelligent observer, upon an instrument not unlike a sieve and that he entered the house by the chimney. Of these conflicting reports, the former was the first to be generally circulated, but the latter, in view of the bizarre presence and eccentric ways of the newest inhabitant, obtained wider credence. By whatever means he arrived, there can be no doubt that he was in, and in possession of the Manse, on the first of May; because on the morning of that day he was inspected by Mrs Morgan ap Lloyd Jones, and subsequently by the numerous persons her report brought up the mountain slope, engaged in the curious occupation of nailing sheet-tin across the void window sockets of his new domicile—'blinding his house', as Mrs Morgan ap Lloyd Jones not inaptly termed it.

He was a small-bodied, sallow faced little man, clad in a close-fitting garment of some stiff, dark material, which

Mr Parry Davies, the Llyddwdd shoemaker, opined was leather. His aquiline nose, thin lips, high cheek-ridges, and pointed chin, were all small and mutually well proportioned; but the bones and muscles of his face were rendered excessively prominent and distinct by his extreme leanness. The same cause contributed to the sunken appearance of the large eager-looking grey eyes, that gazed forth from under his phenomenally wide and high forehead. It was this latter feature that most powerfully attracted the attention of an observer. It seemed to be great beyond all preconceived ratio to the rest of his countenance. Dimensions, corrugations, wrinkles, venation, were alike abnormally exaggerated. Below it his eyes glowed like lights in some cave at a cliff's foot. It so over-powered and suppressed the rest of his face as to give an *unhuman* appearance almost, to what would otherwise have been an unquestionably handsome profile. The lank black hair that hung unkempt before his eyes served to increase rather than conceal this effect, by adding to unnatural altitude a suggestion of hydrocephalic projection: and the idea of something ultra human was furthermore accentuated by the temporal arteries that pulsated visibly through his transparent yellow skin. No wonder, in view even of these things, that among the highly and over-poetical Cymric of Llyddwdd the sieve theory of arrival found considerable favour.

It was his bearing and actions, however, much more than his personality, that won over believers to the warlock notion of matters. In almost every circumstance of life the observant villagers soon found his ways were not only not *their* ways, but altogether inexplicable upon any theory of motives they could conceive. Thus, in a small matter at the beginning, when Arthur Price Williams, eminent and famous in every tavern in Caernarvonshire for his social gifts, endeavoured, in choicest Welsh and even choicer English, to inveigle the stranger into conversation over the sheet-tin performance, he failed utterly. Inquisitional supposition, straightforward enquiry, offer of assistance, suggestion of method, sarcasm, irony, abuse, and at last, gage of battle, though shouted with much effort from the road hedge, went unanswered and apparently unheard. Missile weapons, Arthur Price Williams found, were equally unavailing for the purpose of introduction, and the gathered crowd dispersed with unappeased curiosity and suspicion. Later in the day, the swarth apparition was seen striding down the mountain road towards the village, hatless, and with such swift width of step and set resolution of countenance, that Arthur Price Williams, beholding him from afar from the 'Pig and Whistle' doorway was seized with dire consternation, and hid behind the Dutch oven in the kitchen till he was past. Wild panic also smote the school-house as the children were coming out, and drove them indoors like leaves before a gale. He was merely seeking the provision shop, however, and erupted thencefrom after a prolonged stay, loaded with a various armful of blue parcels, a loaf, herrings, pigs' trotters, salt pork, and a black bottle, with which he returned in the same swift projectile gait to the Manse. His way of shopping was to name, and to name simply, without solitary other word of explanation, civility or request, the article he required.

The shopkeeper's crude meteorological superstitions and inquisitive commonplaces, he seemed not to hear, and he might have been esteemed deaf if he had not evinced the promptest attention to the faintest relevant remark. Consequently it was speedily rumoured that he was determined to avoid all but the most necessary human intercourse. He lived altogether mysteriously, in the decaying manse, without mortal service or companionship, presumably sleeping on planks or litter, and either preparing his own food or eating it raw. This, coupled with the popular conception of the haunting patricides, did much to strengthen the popular supposition of some vast gulf between the newcomer and common humanity. The only thing that was inharmonious with this idea of severance from mankind was a constant flux of crates filled with grotesquely contorted glassware, cases of brazen and steel instruments, huge coils of wire, vast iron and fire-clay implements, of inconceivable purpose, jars and phials labelled in black and scarlet—POISON, huge packages of books, and gargantuan rolls of cartridge paper, which set in towards his Llyddwdd quarters from the outer world. The apparently hieroglyphic inscriptions on these various consignments revealed at the profound scrutiny of Pugh Jones that the style and title of the new inhabitant was Dr Moses Nebogipfel, Ph.D., F.R.S., N.W.R., PAID; at which discovery much edification was felt, especially among the purely Welsh-speaking community. Further than this, these arrivals, by their evident unfitness for any allowable mortal use, and inferential diabolicalness, filled the neighbourhood with a vague horror and lively curiosity, which were greatly augmented by the extraordinary phenomena, and still more extraordinary accounts thereof, that followed their reception in the Manse.

The first of these was on Wednesday, the fifteenth of May, when the Calvinistic Methodists of Llyddwdd had their annual commemoration festival; on which occasion, in accordance with custom, dwellers in the surrounding parishes of Rwstog, Peu-y-garn, Caergyllwdd, Llanrdd, and even distant Llanrwst flocked into the village. Popular thanks to Providence were materialized in the usual way, by means of plumb-bread and butter, mixed tea, *terza*, consecrated flirtations, kiss-in-the-ring, rough-and-tumble football, and vituperative political speechmaking. About half-past eight the fun began to tarnish, and the assembly to break up; and by nine numerous couples and occasional groups were wending their way in the darkling along the hilly Llyddwdd and Rwstog road. It was a calm warm night; one of those nights when lamps, gas and heavy sleep seem stupid ingratitude to the Creator. The zenith sky was an ineffable deep lucent blue, and the evening star hung golden in the liquid darkness of the west. In the north-north-west, a faint phosphorescence marked the sunken day. The moon was just rising, pallid and gibbous over the huge haze-dimmed shoulder of Pen-y-pwll. Against the wan eastern sky, from the vague outline of the mountain slope, the Manse stood out black, clear, and solitary. The stillness of the twilight had hushed the myriad murmurs of the day. Only the sounds of footsteps and voices and laughter, that came fitfully rising and falling from the roadway, and an intermittent hammering in the darkened dwelling, broke the silence. Suddenly a strange whizzing, buzzing whirr filled the night air, and a bright flicker glanced across the dim path of the wayfarers. All eyes were turned in astonishment to the old Manse. The house no longer loomed a black featureless block but was filled to overflowing with light. From the gaping holes in the roof, from chinks and fissures amid tiles and brickwork, from every gap which Nature or man had pierced in the crumbling old shell, a blinding blue-white glare was streaming, beside which the rising moon seemed a disc of opaque sulphur. The thin mist of the dewy night had caught the violet glow and hung, unearthly smoke, over the colourless blaze. A strange turmoil and outcrying in the old Manse now began, and grew ever more audible to the clustering spectators, and therewith came clanging loud impacts against the window-guarding tin. Then from the gleaming roof-gaps of the house suddenly vomited forth a wondrous swarm of heteromerous living things—swallows, sparrows, martins, owls, bats, insects in visible multitudes, to hang for many minutes a noisy, gyring, spreading cloud over the black gables and chimneys, . . . and then slowly to thin out and vanish away in the night.

As this tumult died away the throbbing humming that had first arrested attention grew once more in the listener's hearing, until at last it was the only sound in the long stillness. Presently, however, the road gradually awoke again to the beating and shuffling of feet, as the knots of Rwstog people, one by one, turned their blinking eyes from the dazzling whiteness and, pondering deeply, continued their homeward way.

The cultivated reader will have already discerned that this phenomenon, which sowed a whole crop of uncanny thoughts in the minds of these worthy folk, was simply the installation of the electric light in the Manse. Truly, this last vicissitude of the old house was its strangest one. Its revival to mortal life was like the raising of Lazarus. From that hour forth, by night and day, behind the tin-blinded windows, the tamed lightning illuminated every corner of its quickly changing interior. The almost frenzied energy of the lank-haired, leather-clad little doctor swept away into obscure holes and corners and common destruction, creeper sprays, toadstools, rose leaves, birds' nests, birds' eggs, cobwebs, and all the coatings and lovingly fanciful trimmings with which that maternal old dotard, Dame Nature, had tricked out the decaying house for its lying in state. The magneto-electric apparatus whirred incessantly amid the vestiges of the wainscoted dining-room, where once the eighteenth century tenant had piously read morning prayer and eaten his Sunday dinner; and in the place of his sacred symbolical sideboard was a nasty heap of coke. The oven of the bakehouse supplied substratum and material for a forge, whose snorting, panting bellows, and intermittent, ruddy, spark-laden blast made the benighted, but Bible-lit Welsh women murmur in liquid Cymric, as they hurried by: 'Whose breath kindleth coals, and out of his mouth is a flame of fire.' For the idea these good people formed of it was that a tame, but occasionally restive, leviathan had been added to the terrors of the haunted house. The constantly increasing accumulation of pieces of machinery, big brass castings, block tin, casks, crates, and packages of innumerable articles, by their demands for space, necessitated the sacrifice of most of the slighter partitions of the house; and the beams and flooring of the upper chambers were also mercilessly sawn away by the tireless scientist in such a way as to convert them into mere shelves and corner brackets of the atrial space between cellars and rafters. Some of the sounder planking was utilized in the making of a rude broad table, upon which files and heaps of geometrical diagrams speedily accumulated. The production of these latter seemed to be the object upon which the mind of Dr Nebogipfel was so inflexibly set. All other circumstances of his life were made entirely subsidiary to this one occupation. Strangely complicated traceries of lines they were—plans, elevations, sections by surfaces and solids, that, with the help of logarithmic mechanical apparatus and involved curvigraphical machines, spread swiftly under his expert hands over yard after yard of paper. Some of these symbolized shapes he despatched to London, and they presently returned, *realized*, in forms of brass and ivory, and nickel and mahogany. Some of them he himself translated into solid models of metal and wood; occasionally casting the metallic ones in moulds of sand, but often laboriously hewing them out of the block for greater precision of dimension. In this second process, among other appliances, he employed a steel circular saw set with diamond powder and made to rotate with extraordinary swiftness, by means of steam and multiplying gear. It was this latter thing, more than all else, that filled Llyddwdd with a sickly loathing of the Doctor as a man of blood and darkness. Often in the silence of midnight—for the newest inhabitant heeded the sun but little in his incessant research—the awakened dwellers around Pen-y-pwll would hear, what was at first a complaining murmur, like the groaning of a wounded man, '*gurr*-urr-urr-URR', rising by slow gradations in pitch and intensity to the likeness of a voice in despairing passionate protest, and at last ending abruptly in a sharp piercing shriek that rang in the ears for hours afterwards and begot numberless grewsome dreams.

The mystery of all these unearthly noises and inexplicable phenomena, the Doctor's inhumanly brusque bearing and evident uneasiness when away from his absorbing occupation, his entire and jealous seclusion, and his terrifying behaviour to certain officious intruders, roused popular resentment and curiosity to the highest, and a plot was already on foot to make some sort of popular inquisition (probably accompanied by an experimental ducking) into his proceedings, when the sudden death of the hunchback Hughes in a fit, brought matters to an unexpected crisis. It happened in broad daylight, in the roadway just opposite the Manse. Half a dozen people witnessed it. The unfortunate creature was seen to fall suddenly and roll about on the pathway, struggling violently, as it appeared to the spectators, with some invisible assailant. When assistance reached him he was purple in the face and his blue lips were covered with a glairy foam. He died almost as soon as they laid hands on him.

Owen Thomas, the general practitioner, vainly assured the excited crowd which speedily gathered outside the 'Pig and Whistle', whither the body had been carried, that death was unquestionably natural. A horrible zymotic suspicion had gone forth that deceased was the victim of Dr Nebogipfel's imputed aerial powers. The contagion was with the news that passed like a flash through the village and set all Llyddwdd seething with a fierce desire for action against the worker of this iniquity. Downright superstition, which had previously walked somewhat modestly about the village, in the fear of ridicule and the Doctor, now appeared boldly before the sight of all men, clad in the terrible majesty of truth. People who had hitherto kept entire silence as to their fears of the imp-like philosopher suddenly discovered a fearsome pleasure in whispering dread possibilities to kindred souls, and from whispers of possibilities their sympathy-fostered utterances soon developed into unhesitating asserverations in loud and even high-pitched tones. The fancy of a captive leviathan, already alluded to, which had up to now been the horrid but secret joy of a certain conclave of ignorant old women, was published to all the world as indisputable fact; it being stated, on her own authority, that the animal had, on one occasion, chased Mrs Morgan ap Lloyd Jones almost into Rwstog. The story that Nebogipfel had been heard within the Manse chanting, in conjunction with the Williamses, horrible blasphemy, and that a 'black flapping thing, of the size of a young calf', had thereupon entered the gap in the roof, was universally believed in. A grisly anecdote, that owed its origination to a stumble in the churchyard, was circulated, to the effect that the Doctor had been caught ghoulishly tearing with his long white fingers at a new-made grave. The numerously attested declaration that Nebogipfel and the murdered Williams had been seen hanging the sons on a ghostly gibbet, at the back of the house, was due to the electric illumination of a fitfully wind-shaken tree. A hundred like stories hurtled thickly about the village and darkened the moral atmosphere. The Reverend Elijah Ulysses Cook, hearing of the tumult, sallied forth to allay it, and narrowly escaped drawing on himself the gathering lightning.

By eight o'clock (it was Monday the twenty-second of July) a grand demonstration had organized itself against the 'necromancer'. A number of bolder hearts among the men formed the nucleus of the gathering, and at nightfall Arthur Price Williams, John Peters, and others brought torches and raised their spark-raining flames aloft with curt ominous suggestions. The less adventurous village manhood came straggling late to the rendezvous, and with them the married women came in groups of four or five, greatly increasing the excitement of the assembly with their shrill hysterical talk and active imaginations. After these the children and young girls, overcome by undefinable dread, crept quietly out of the too silent and shadowy houses into the yellow glare of the pine knots, and the tumultuary noise of the thickening people. By nine, nearly half the Llyddwdd population was massed before the 'Pig and Whistle'. There was a confused murmur of many tongues, but above all the stir and chatter of the growing crowd could be heard the coarse, cracked voice of the blood-thirsty old fanatic, Pritchard, drawing a congenial lesson from the fate of the four hundred and fifty idolators of Carmel.

Just as the church clock was beating out the hour, an occultly originated movement up hill began, and soon the whole assembly, men, women, and children, was moving in a fear-compacted mass, towards the ill-fated doctor's abode. As they left the brightly-lit public house behind them, a quavering female voice began singing one of those grim-sounding canticles that so satisfy the Calvinistic ear. In a wonderfully short time, the tune had been caught up, first by two or three, and then by the whole procession, and the manifold shuffling of heavy shoon grew swiftly into rhythm with the beats of the hymn. When, however, their goal rose, like a blazing star, over the undulation of the road, the volume of the chanting suddenly died away, leaving only the voices of the ringleaders, shouting indeed now somewhat out of tune, but, if anything, more vigorously than before. Their persistence and example nevertheless failed to prevent a perceptible breaking and slackening of the pace, as the Manse was neared, and when the gate was reached, the whole crowd came to a dead halt. Vague fear for the future had begotten the courage that had brought the villagers thus far: fear for the present now smothered its kindred birth. The intense blaze from the gaps in the death-like silent pile lit up rows of livid, hesitating faces: and a smothered, frightened sobbing broke out among the children. 'Well,' said Arthur Price Williams, addressing Jack Peters, with an expert assumption of modest discipleship, 'what do we do *now*, Jack?' But Peters was regarding the Manse with manifest dubiety, and ignored the question. The Llyddwdd witch-find seemed to be suddenly aborting.

At this juncture old Pritchard suddenly pushed his way forward, gesticulating weirdly with his bony hands and long arms. '*What!*' he shouted, in broken notes, 'fear ye to smite when the Lord hateth? *Burn* the warlock!' And seizing a flambeau from Peters, he flung open the rickety gate and strode on down the drive, his torch leaving a coiling trail of scintillant sparks on the night wind. 'Burn the warlock,' screamed a shrill voice from the wavering crowd, and in a moment the gregarious human instinct had prevailed. With an outburst of incoherent, threatening voice, the mob poured after the fanatic.

Woe betide the Philosopher now! They expected barricaded doors; but with a groan of conscious insufficiency, the hinge-rusted portals swung wide at the push of Pritchard. Blinded by the light, he hesitated for a second on the threshold, while his followers came crowding up behind him.

Those who were there say that they saw Dr Nebogipfel, standing in the toneless electric glare, on a peculiar erection of brass and ebony and ivory; and that he seemed to be smiling at them, half pityingly and half scornfully, as it is said martyrs are wont to smile. Some assert, moreover, that by his side was sitting a tall man, clad in ravenswing, and some even aver that this second man—whom others deny— bore on his face the likeness of the Reverend Elijah Ulysses Cook, while others declare that he resembled the description of the murdered Williams. Be that as it may, it must now go unproven for ever, for suddenly a wondrous thing smote the crowd as it swarmed in through the entrance. Pritchard pitched headlong on the floor senseless. Wild shouts and shrieks of anger, changed in mid utterance to yells of agonizing fear, or to the mute gasp of heart-stopping horror: and then a frantic rush was made for the doorway.

For the calm, smiling doctor, and his quiet, black-clad companion, and the polished platform which upbore them, had vanished before their eyes!

How an Esoteric Story became Possible

A silvery-foliaged willow by the side of a mere. Out of the cress-spangled waters below, rise clumps of sedge-blades, and among them glows the purple fleur-de-lys, and sapphire vapour of forget-me-nots. Beyond is a sluggish stream of water reflecting the intense blue of the moist Fenland sky; and beyond that a low osier-fringed eyot. This limits all the visible universe, save some scattered pollards and spear-like poplars showing against the violet distance. At the foot of the willow reclines the Author watching a copper butterfly fluttering from iris to iris.

Who can fix the colours of the sunset? Who can take a cast of flame? Let him essay to register the mutations of mortal thought as it wanders from a copper butterfly to the disembodied soul, and thence passes to spiritual motions and the vanishing of Dr Moses Nebogipfel and the Rev. Elijah Ulysses Cook from the world of sense.

As the author lay basking there and speculating, as another once did under the Budh tree, on mystic transmutations, a presence became apparent. There was a somewhat on the eyot between him and the purple horizon—an opaque reflecting entity, making itself dimly perceptible by reflection in the water to his averted eyes. He raised them in curious surprise.

What was it?

He stared in stupefied astonishment at the apparition, doubted, blinked, rubbed his eyes, stared again, and believed. It was solid, it cast a shadow, and it upbore two men. There was white metal in it that blazed in the noontide sun like incandescent magnesium, ebony bars that drank in the light, and white parts that gleamed like polished ivory. Yet withal it seemed unreal. The thing was not square as a machine ought to be, but all awry: it was twisted and seemed falling over, hanging in two directions, as those queer crystals called triclinic hang; it seemed like a machine that had been crushed or warped; it was suggestive and not confirmatory, like the machine of a disordered dream. The men, too, were dreamlike. One was short, intensely sallow, with a strangely-shaped head, and clad in a garment of dark olive green; the other was, grotesquely out of place, evidently a clergyman of the Established Church, a fair-haired, pale-faced respectable-looking man.

Once more doubt came rushing in on the author. He sprawled back and stared at the sky, rubbed his eyes, stared at the willow wands that hung between him and the blue, closely examined his hands to see if his eyes had any new things to relate about them, and then sat up again and stared at the eyot. A gentle breeze stirred the osiers; a white bird was flapping its way through the lower sky. The machine of the vision had vanished! It was an illusion—a projection of the subjective—an assertion of the immateriality of mind. 'Yes,' interpolated the sceptic faculty, 'but *how comes it that the clergyman is still there?*'

The clergyman had not vanished. In intense perplexity the author examined this black-coated phenomenon as he stood regarding the world with hand-shaded eyes. The author knew the periphery of that eyot by heart, and the question that troubled him was, 'Whence?' The clergyman looked as Frenchmen look when they land at Newhaven— intensely travel-worn; his clothes showed rubbed and seamy in the bright day. When he came to the edge of the island and shouted a question to the author, his voice was broken and trembled. 'Yes,' answered the author, 'it is an island. *How did you get there?*'

But the clergyman, instead of replying to this asked a very strange question.

He said 'Are you in the nineteenth century?' The author made him repeat that question before he replied. 'Thank heaven,' cried the clergyman rapturously. Then he asked very eagerly for the exact date.

'August the ninth, eighteen hundred and eighty-seven,' he repeated after the author. 'Heaven be praised!' and sinking down on the eyot so that the sedges hid him, he audibly burst into tears.

Now the author was mightily surprised at all this, and going a certain distance along the mere, he obtained a punt, and getting into it he hastily poled to the eyot where he had last seen the clergyman. He found him lying insensible among the reeds, and carried him in his punt to the house where he lived, and the clergyman lay there insensible for ten days.

Meanwhile, it became known that he was the Rev. Elijah

Cook, who had disappeared from Llyddwdd with Dr Moses Nebogipfel three weeks before.

On August 19th, the nurse called the author out of his study to speak to the invalid. He found him perfectly sensible, but his eyes were strangely bright, and his face was deadly pale. 'Have you found out who I am?' he asked.

'You are the Rev. Elijah Ulysses Cook, Master of Arts, of Pembroke College, Oxford, and Rector of Llyddwdd, near Rwstog, in Caernarvon.'

He bowed his head. 'Have you been told anything of how I came here?'

'I found you among the reeds,' I said. He was silent and thoughtful for a while. 'I have a deposition to make. Will you take it? It concerns the murder of an old man named Williams, which occurred in 1862, this disappearance of Dr Moses Nebogipfel, the abduction of a ward in the year 4003——'

The author stared.

'The year of our Lord 4003,' he corrected. 'She would come. Also several assaults on public officials in the years 17,901 and 2.'

The author coughed.

'The years 17,901 and 2, and valuable medical, social, and physiographical data for all time.'

After a consultation with the doctor, it was decided to have the deposition taken down, and this is which constitutes the remainder of the story of the Chronic Argonauts.

On August 29th 1887, the Rev. Elijah Cook died. His body was conveyed to Llyddwdd, and buried in the churchyard there.

Part II

The Esoteric Story Based on the Clergyman's Depositions

The Anachronic Man

Incidentally it has been remarked in the first part, how the Reverend Elijah Ulysses Cook attempted and failed to quiet the superstitious excitement of the villagers on the afternoon of the memorable twenty-second of July. His next proceeding was to try and warn the unsocial philosopher of the dangers which impended. With this intent he made his way from the rumour-pelted village, through the silent, slumbrous heat of the July afternoon, up the slopes of Pen-y-pwll, to the old Manse. His loud knocking at the heavy door called forth dull resonance from the interior, and produced a shower of lumps of plaster and fragments of decaying touchwood from the rickety porch, but beyond this the dreamy stillness of the summer mid-day remained unbroken. Everything was so quiet as he stood there expectant, that the occasional speech of the haymakers a mile away in the fields, over towards Rwstog, could be distinctly heard. The reverend gentleman waited long, then knocked again, and waited again, and listened, until the echoes and the patter of rubbish had melted away into the deep silence, and the creeping in the blood-vessels of his ears had become oppressively audible, swelling and sinking with sounds like the confused murmuring of a distant crowd, and causing a suggestion of anxious discomfort to spread slowly over his mind.

Again he knocked, this time loud, quick blows with his stick, and almost immediately afterwards, leaning his hand against the door, he kicked its panels vigorously. There was a shouting of echoes, a protesting jarring of hinges, and then the oaken door yawned and displayed, in the blue blaze of the electric light, vestiges of partitions, piles of planking and straw, masses of metal, heaps of papers and overthrown apparatus, to the rector's astonished eyes. 'Doctor Nebogipfel, excuse my intruding,' he called out, but the only response was a reverberation among the black beams and shadows that hung dimly above. For almost a minute he stood there, leaning forward over the threshold, staring at the glittering mechanisms, diagrams, books, scattered indiscriminately with broken food, packing cases, heaps of coke, hay, and microcosmic lumber, about the undivided house cavity; and then, removing his hat and treading stealthily, as if the silence were a sacred thing, he stepped into the apparently deserted shelter of the Doctor.

His eyes sought everywhere, as he cautiously made his way through the confusion, with a strange anticipation of finding Nebogipfel hidden somewhere in the sharp black shadows among the litter, so strong in him was an indescribable sense of a perceiving presence. This feeling was so vivid that, when, after an abortive exploration, he seated himself upon Nebogipfel's diagram-covered bench, it made him explain in a forced hoarse voice to the stillness—'He is not here. I have something to say to him. I must wait for him.' It was so vivid, too, that the trickling of some grit down the wall in the vacant corner behind him made him start round in a sudden perspiration. There was nothing visible there, but turning his head back, he was stricken rigid with horror by the swift, noiseless apparition of Nebogipfel, ghastly pale, and with red stained hands, crouching upon a strange-looking metallic platform, and with his deep grey eyes looking intently into the visitor's face.

Cook's first impulse was to yell out his fear, but his throat was paralysed, and he could only stare fascinated at the bizarre countenance that had thus clashed suddenly into visibility. The lips were quivering and the breath came in short convulsive sobs. The un-human forehead was wet with perspiration, while the veins were swollen, knotted and purple. The Doctor's red hands, too, he noticed, were trembling, as the hands of slight people tremble after intense muscular exertion, and his lips closed and opened as if he, too, had a difficulty in speaking as he gasped, 'Who—what do you do here?'

Cook answered not a word, but stared with hair erect, open mouth, and dilated eyes, at the dark red unmistakeable smear that streaked the pure ivory and gleaming nickel and shining ebony of the platform.

'What are you doing here?' repeated the doctor, raising himself. 'What do you want?'

Cook gave a convulsive effort. 'In Heaven's name, *what* are you?' he gasped; and then black curtains came closing in from every side, sweeping the squatting, dwarfish phantasm that reeled before him into rayless, voiceless night.

★   ★   ★

The Reverend Elijah Ulysses Cook recovered his perceptions to find himself lying on the floor of the old Manse, and Doctor Nebogipfel, no longer blood-stained and with all trace of his agitation gone, kneeling by his side and bending over him with a glass of brandy in his hand. 'Do not be alarmed, sir,' said the philosopher with a faint smile, as the clergyman opened his eyes. 'I have not treated you to a disembodied spirit, or anything nearly so extraordinary ... May I offer you this?'

The clergyman submitted quietly to the brandy, and then stared perplexed into Nebogipfel's face, vainly searching his memory for what occurrences had preceded his insensibility. Raising himself at last into a sitting posture, he saw the oblique mass of metals that had appeared with the doctor, and immediately all that happened flashed back upon his mind. He looked from this structure to the recluse, and from the recluse to the structure.

'There is absolutely no deception, sir,' said Nebogipfel with the slightest trace of mockery in his voice. 'I lay no claim to work in matters spiritual. It is a *bona fide* mechanical contrivance, a thing emphatically of this sordid world. Excuse me—just one minute.' He rose from his knees, stepped upon the mahogany platform, took a curiously curved lever in his hand and pulled it over. Cook rubbed his eyes. *There* certainly was no deception. The doctor and the machine had vanished.

The reverend gentleman felt no horror this time, only a slight nervous shock, to see the doctor presently re-appear 'in the twinkling of an eye' and get down from the machine. From that he walked in a straight line with his hands behind his back and his face downcast, until his progress was stopped by the intervention of a circular saw; then, turning round sharply on his heel, he said:

'I was thinking while I was . . . away . . . Would you like to come? I should greatly value a companion.'

The clergyman was still sitting, hatless, on the floor. 'I am afraid,' he said slowly, 'you will think me stupid——'

'Not at all,' interrupted the doctor. 'The stupidity is mine. You desire to have all this explained . . . wish to know where I am going first. I have spoken so little with men of this age for the last ten years or more that I have ceased to make due allowances and concessions for other minds. I will do my best, but that I fear will be very unsatisfactory. It is a long story . . . Do you find that floor comfortable to sit on? If not, there is a nice packing case over there, or some straw behind you, or this bench—the diagrams are done with now, but I am afraid of the drawing pins. You may sit on the Chronic Argo!'

'*No*, thank you,' slowly replied the clergyman, eyeing that deformed structure thus indicated, suspiciously; 'I am *quite* comfortable here.'

'Then I will begin. Do you read fables? Modern ones?'

'I am afraid I must confess to a good deal of fiction,' said the clergyman depreciatingly. 'In Wales the ordained ministers of the sacraments of the Church have perhaps *too* large a share of leisure——'

'Have you read the Ugly Duckling?'

'Hans Christian Andersen's—yes—in my childhood.'

'A wonderful story—a story that has even been full of tears and heart swelling hopes for me, since first it came to me in my lonely boyhood and saved me from unspeakable things. That story, if you understand it well, will tell you almost all that you should know of me to comprehend how that machine came to be thought of in a mortal brain . . . Even when I read that simple narrative for the first time, a thousand bitter experiences had begun the teaching of my isolation among the people of my birth—I knew the story was for me. The ugly duckling that proved to be a swan, that lived through all contempt and bitterness, to float at last sublime. From that hour forth, I dreamt of meeting with my kind, dreamt of encountering that sympathy I knew was my profoundest need. Twenty years I lived in that hope, lived and worked, lived and wandered, loved even, and, at last, despaired. Only once among all those millions of wondering, astonished, indifferent, contemptuous, and insidious faces that I met with in that passionate wandering, looked *one* upon me as I desired . . . looked——'

He paused. The Reverend Cook glanced up into his face, expecting some indication of the deep feeling that had sounded in his last words. It was downcast, clouded, and thoughtful, but the mouth was rigidly firm.

'In short, Mr Cook, I discovered that I was one of those superior Cagots called a genius—a man born out of my time—a man thinking the thoughts of a wiser age, doing things and believing things that men now *cannot* understand, and that in the years ordained to me there was nothing but silence and suffering for my soul—unbroken solitude, man's bitterest pain. I knew I was an Anachronic Man; my age was still to come. One filmy hope alone held me to life, a hope to which I clung until it had become a certain thing. Thirty years of unremitting toil and deepest thought among the hidden things of matter and form and life, and then *that*, the Chronic Argo, *the ship that sails through time*, and now I go to join my generation, to journey through the ages till my time has come.'

The Chronic Argo

Dr Nebogipfel paused, looking in sudden doubt at the clergyman's perplexed face. 'You think that sounds mad,' he said, 'to travel through time?'

'It certainly jars with accepted opinions,' said the clergyman, allowing the faintest suggestion of controversy to appear in his intonation, and speaking apparently to the Chronic Argo. Even clergyman of the Church of England you see can have a suspicion of illusions at times.

'It certainly *does* jar with accepted opinions,' agreed the philosopher cordially. 'It does more than that—it defies accepted opinions to mortal combat. Opinions of all sorts, Mr Cook,—Scientific Theories, Laws, Articles of Belief, or, to come to elements, Logical Premises, Ideas, or whatever you like to call them,—all are, from the infinite nature of things, so many diagrammatic caricatures of the ineffable,— caricatures altogether to be avoided save where they are necessary in the shaping of results—as chalk outlines are necessary to the painter and plans and sections to the engineer. Men, from the exigencies of their being, find this hard to believe.'

The Rev. Elijah Ulysses Cook nodded his head with the quiet smile of one whose opponent has unwittingly given a point.

'It is as easy to come to regard ideas as complete reproductions of entities as it is to roll off a log. Hence it is that almost all civilized men believe in the *reality* of the Greek geometrical conceptions.'

'Oh! pardon me, sir,' interrupted Cook. 'Most men know that a geometrical point has no existence in matter, and the same with a geometrical line. I think you underrate . . .'

'Yes, yes, *those* things are recognized,' said Nebogipfel calmly; 'but now . . . a cube. Does that exist in the material universe?'

'Certainly.'

'An instantaneous cube?'

'I don't know what you intend by that expression.'

'Without any other sort of extension; a body having length, breadth, and thickness, exists?'

'What other sort of extension *can* there be?' asked Cook, with raised eyebrows.

'Has it never occurred to you that no form can exist in the material universe that has no extension in time? . . . Has it never glimmered upon your consciousness that nothing stood between men and a geometry of four dimensions— length, breadth, thickness, and *duration*—but the inertia of opinion, the impulse from the Levantine philosophers of the bronze age?'

'Putting it that way,' said the clergyman, 'it does look as though there was a flaw somewhere in the notion of tridimensional being; *but* . . .' He became silent, leaving that sufficiently eloquent 'but' to convey all the prejudice and distrust that filled his mind.

'When we take up this new light of a fourth dimension and re-examine our physical science in its illumination,' continued Nebogipfel, after a pause, 'we find ourselves no longer limited by hopeless restriction to a certain beat of time—to our own generation. Locomotion along lines of duration—chronic navigation comes within the range, first, of geometrical theory, and then of practical mechanics. There *was* a time when men could only move horizontally and in their appointed country. The clouds floated above them unattainable things, mysterious chariots of those fearful gods who dwelt among the mountain summits. Speaking practically, man in those days was restricted to motion in two dimensions; and even there circumambient ocean and hypoborean fear bound him in. But those times were to pass away. First, the keel of Jason cut its way between the Symplegades, and then in the fulness of time, Columbus dropped anchor in a bay of Atlantis. Then man burst his bidimensional limits, and invaded the third dimension, soaring with Montgolfier into the clouds, and sinking with the diving bell into the purple treasure-caves of the waters. And now another step, and the hidden past and unknown future are before us. We stand upon a mountain summit with the plains of the ages spread below.'

Nebogipfel paused and looked down at his hearer.

The Reverend Elijah Cook was sitting with an expression of strong distrust on his face. Preaching much had brought home certain truths to him very vividly, and he always suspected rhetoric. 'Are those things figures of speech,' he asked; 'or am I to take them as precise statements? Do you speak of travelling through time in the same way as one might speak of Omnipotence making His pathway on the storm, or do you—a—mean what you say?'

Dr Nebogipfel smiled quietly. 'Come and look at these diagrams,' he said, and then with elaborate simplicity he commenced to explain again to the clergyman the new quadridimensional geometry. Insensibly Cook's aversion passed away, and seeming impossibility grew possible, now that such tangible things as diagrams and models could be brought forward in evidence. Presently he found himself asking questions, and his interest grew deeper and deeper as Nebogipfel slowly and with precise clearness unfolded the beautiful order of his strange invention. The moments slipped away unchecked, as the Doctor passed on to the narrative of his research, and it was with a start of surprise that the clergyman noticed the deep blue of the dying twilight through the open doorway.

'The voyage,' said Nebogipfel concluding his history, 'will be full of un-dreamt of dangers—already in one brief essay I have stood in the very jaws of death—but it is also full of the divinest promise of undreamt-of joy. Will you come? Will you walk among the people of the Golden Years? . . .'

But the mention of death by the philosopher had brought flooding back to the mind of Cook, all the horrible sensations of that first apparition.

'Dr Nebogipfel . . . one question?' He hesitated. 'On your hands . . . *Was it blood?*'

Nebogipfel's countenance fell. He spoke slowly.

'When I had stopped my machine, I found myself in this room as it used to be. *Hark!*'

'It is the wind in the trees towards Rwstog.'

'It sounded like the voices of a multitude of people singing . . . When I had stopped I found myself in this room as it used to be. An old man, a young man, and a lad were sitting at a table—reading some book together. I stood behind them unsuspected. "Evil spirits assailed him," read the old man; "but it is written, 'to him that overcometh

212

shall be given life eternal.' They came as entreating friends, but he endured through all their snares. They came as principalities and powers, but he defied them in the name of the King of Kings. Once even it is told that in his study, while he was translating the New Testament into German, the Evil One himself appeared before him . . ." Just then the lad glanced timorously round, and with a fearful wail fainted away . . .'

'The others sprang at me . . . It was a fearful grapple . . . The old man clung to my throat, screaming "Man or Devil, I defy thee . . ." '

'I could not help it. We rolled together on the floor . . . the knife his trembling son had dropped came to my hand . . . *Hark!*'

He paused and listened, but Cook remained staring at him in the same horror-stricken attitude he had assumed when the memory of the blood-stained hands had rushed back over his mind.

'Do you hear what they are crying? *Hark!*'
Burn the warlock! Burn the murderer!
'Do you hear? There is no time to be lost.'
Slay the murderer of cripples. Kill the devil's claw!
'Come! Come!'

Cook, with a convulsive effort, made a gesture of repugnance and strode to the doorway. A crowd of black figures roaring towards him in the red torchlight made him recoil. He shut the door and faced Nebogipfel.

The thin lips of the Doctor curled with a contemptuous sneer. 'They will kill you if you stay,' he said; and seizing his unresisting visitor by the wrist, he forced him towards the glittering machine. Cook sat down and covered his face with his hands.

In another moment the door was flung open, and old Pritchard stood blinking on the threshold.

A pause. A hoarse shout changing suddenly into a sharp shrill shriek.

A thunderous roar like the bursting forth of a great fountain of water.

The voyage of the Chronic Argonauts had begun.

End of Part II of the Chronic Argonauts

How did it end? How came it that Cook wept with joy to return once more to this nineteenth century of ours? Why did not Nebogipfel remain with him? All that, and more also, has been written, and will or will never be read, according as Fate may have decreed to the Curious Reader.

Published serially in
The Science Schools Journal,
April, May and June 1888

NOTES

CHAPTER I

[1] *The Works of Oscar Wilde* (ed. G. F. Maine), 1948, p. 895.

[2] *Last Letters of Aubrey Beardsley* (ed. John Gray), 1904, p. 26.

[3] Ibid., pp. 107–8.

[4] A number of refutations of Nordau subsequently appeared, the most celebrated being an extended review by Bernard Shaw (published in book form in 1908 as *The Sanity of Art*).

[5] *Degeneration*, 1895, p. 2.

[6] Nordau, op. cit., pp. 5–6.

[7] Translated by Robert Baldick (Penguin Classics), 1959, pp. 219–20.

[8] *The Works of Friedrich Nietzsche*, 1895, XI, xiii.

[9] Nevertheless, we also find this identification in Shaw, particularly in *Man and Superman*.

[10] *The Quintessence of Ibsenism*, 1891, p. 2.

[11] Nordau, op. cit., p. 14.

[12] *H. G. Wells*, 1915, p. 18.

[13] *Arnold Bennett and H. G. Wells* (ed. Harris Wilson), 1960, p. 34.

[14] *The Living Novel*, 1946, p. 120.

[15] *First Essays on Literature*, 1923, p. 158.

[16] In *The Rise of the Novel*, 1957, pp. 60–92.

[17] See, for instance, Jolande Jacobi, *The Psychology of C. G. Jung*, 1951, p. 127; C. G. Jung, *Flying Saucers*, 1959.

[18] *Experiment in Autobiography*, 1934, II, 654.

CHAPTER II

[1] 1891 in fact.

[2] Grant Richards, *Memories of a Misspent Youth*, 1932, pp. 327–8.

[3] *The Desert Daisy* (ed. Gordon N. Ray), Urbana, Illinois, 1957.

[4] Geoffrey West (Geoffrey H. Wells), *H. G. Wells: A Sketch for a Portrait*, 1930, p. 45.

[5] See G. West, op. cit., pp. 287–9, for a full account.

[6] G. West, op. cit., p. 67.

[7] *Experiment in Autobiography*, 1934, I, 309.

[8] Ibid., I, 309.

[9] Ibid., I, 114, 138.

[10] *Royal College of Science Magazine* (formerly *Science Schools Journal*), April 1903, p. 221.

[11] *Science Schools Journal*, April 1887, p. 149.

[12] Ibid., p. 151.

[13] *The Works of Oscar Wilde*, 1948, p. 197.

[14] Van Wyck Brooks, *The World of H. G. Wells*, New York, 1915, p. 34.

[15] *Pall Mall Magazine*, September 1895, pp. 153–5.

[16] W. B. Pitkin, 'Time and Pure Activity', *Journal of Philosophy, Psychology and Scientific Methods*, xi (1914), 521–6.

[17] See Frank Kermode, *Romantic Image*, 1957, pp. 1–30.

[18] *Experiment in Autobiography*, I, 309.

[19] See G. West, op. cit., p. 111; Gordon S. Haight, 'H. G. Wells's "The Man of the Year Million",' *Nineteenth Century Fiction*, xii (1958), 323–6.

[20] *Certain Personal Matters*, 1898 [1897], p. 161.

[21] Ibid., p. 167.

[22] Ibid., p. 169.

[23] '1,000,000 A.D.', *Punch*, 25 November 1893.

[24] G. West, op. cit., pp. 291–2.

[25] Manuscript letter (University of Illinois Library).

[26] *Experiment in Autobiography*, I, 396.

[27] For an account of the textual differences between these versions see my article 'The Publication of *The Time Machine* 1894–5.' *Review of English Studies*, n.s., xi (1960), 42–51.

[28] Quoted by G. West, op. cit., p. 102.

[29] *Review of Reviews*, xi (1895), 263.

[30] Ibid., p. 346, p. 416.

[31] See Grant Richards, *Memories of a Misspent Youth*, 1932, p. 158; Frederic Whyte, *William Heinemann*, 1928, p. 131; Kennedy Williamson, *W. E. Henley*, 1930, p. 219.

[32] 'The Latest Apocalypse of the End of the World', *Review of Reviews*, xvii (1898), 389–96.

[33] 27 July 1895, p. 3.

[34] *Bookman*, viii (1895), 134–5.

[35] *The Living Novel*, 1946, pp. 119–20.

[36] Edward Shanks, *First Essays on Literature*, 1923, p. 158.

[37] Ibid., p. 160.

[38] *Anatomy of Criticism*, Princeton, 1957, pp. 202–3.

[39] *To-day*, 11 September 1897, p. 164.

[40] Review of *The Plattner Story*, *Athenaeum*, 26 June 1897.

[41] Report of a debate, *Science Schools Journal*, February 1889, p. 153.

[42] Haight, op. cit., p. 325.

[43] It is also significant that the Traveller's first impression of the future world is dominated by the statue of the White Sphinx, and that the first edition of *The Time Machine* had a sphinx upon the cover. The sphinx was a familiar object in *fin de siècle* iconography: *vide* Wilde's poem, 'The Sphinx', published in 1894, and various references in *A Rebours*; also Gustave Moreau's celebrated 'sphinx' paintings, described by Mario Praz in *The Romantic Agony*, Chapter V.

[44] Pritchett, op. cit., p. 119.

[45] Pritchett, op. cit., p. 120.

[46] Frye, op. cit., p. 150.

[47] See Christopher Caudwell, *Studies in a Dying Culture*, 1938, pp. 73–95; A. L. Morton, *The English Utopia*, 1952, pp. 183–94.

[48] 27 July 1895, p. 3.

[49] *Degeneration*, 1895, p. 2.

CHAPTER III

[1] 'The Literature of the Future', *Pall Mall Gazette*, 11 October 1893.

[2] *Experiment in Autobiography*, II, 514.

[3] *The Country of the Blind and Other Stories*, 1911, p. iv.

[4] *The Great God Pan and the Inmost Light*, 1894, pp. 6–7.

[5] Ibid., p. 15.

[6] *Anticipations*, 1901, p. 191.

[7] *Arnold Bennett and H. G. Wells* (ed. Harris Wilson), 1960, p. 59.

[8] *Experiment in Autobiography*, I, 409.

[9] See R. W. Weeks, 'Disentanglement as a Theme in H. G. Wells's Fiction', *Papers of the Michigan Academy of Science, Arts and Letters*, xxxix (1954), 439–44.

CHAPTER IV

[1] *Review of Reviews*, xii (1895), 375; *Daily Chronicle*, 9 October 1895, p. 3.

[2] *Works* (Atlantic Edition, 1924), I, xxi; II, ix.

[3] *Daily Telegraph*, 27 September 1895, p. 8.

[4] *The Puritan*, i (1899), 219.

[5] John Ruskin, *Works* (1907), XXVIII, 154.

[6] Georges Connes, *Etude sur la Pensée de Wells*, Paris, 1926, p. 214.

[7] *Fortnightly Review*, lvi (1891), 111.

[8] *Experiment in Autobiography*, I, 401.

[9] *The Times*, 17 June 1896, p. 17.

[10] *Athenaeum*, 9 May 1896, p. 615.

[11] *Speaker*, 18 April 1896, p. 430.

[12] *Saturday Review*, 11 April 1896, p. 368.

[13] *Saturday Review*, 7 November 1896, p. 497.

[14] *The Young Man*, August 1897, p. 256.

[15] *Guardian*, 3 June 1896, p. 871.

[16] *Works* (Atlantic Edition, 1924), II, ix.

[17] *Idler*, June 1896, p. 724.

[18] *Academy*, 30 May 1896, p. 444.

[19] *Critical Quarterly*, i (1959), 37.

[20] *Works* (Atlantic Edition, 1924), II, ix.

[21] *Saturday Review*, 19 January 1895.

[22] *Bookman*, xlvi (1914), 16.

[23] *Romanes Lectures 1892–1900*, 1900, p. 116.

[24] *Spectator*, 11 April 1896, p. 520.

[25] *Principles and Persuasions*, 1958, p. 10.

[26] Huxley, op. cit., pp. 95–6.

[27] Apparently some of the early chapters of *The War of the Worlds* had been written by March 1896; see *Experiment in Autobiography*, II, 555.

[28] 'Realism v. Romance', *Today*, 11 September 1897, p. 165.

[29] *Bookman*, xiii (1897), 19.

[30] *Saturday Review*, 18 September 1897.

[31] T. S. Eliot, *Selected Essays*, 1953, p. 123.

[32] Norman Nicholson, *H. G. Wells*, 1950, p. 38.

[33] G. K. Chesterton, *Heretics*, 1905, p. 85.

[34] *Works* (Atlantic Edition), V, ix.

[35] *Joseph Conrad: Life and Letters* (ed. G. Jean-Aubry, 1927), I, 259.

CHAPTER V

[1] *Speaker*, 5 February 1898, p. 174.

[2] *Academy* (Supplement), 29 January 1898, p. 121.

[3] *Spectator*, 29 January 1898, p. 168.

[4] *Bookman*, xiii (1898), 183.

[5] *Athenaeum*, 5 February 1898, p. 178.

[6] See Patrick Moore, *Science and Fiction*, 1957, pp. 13–42.

[7] Report of a debate, *Science Schools Journal*, November 1888, p. 58.

[8] *Strand Magazine*, lix (1920), 154.

[9] *Experiment in Autobiography*, II, 543.

[10] Quoted by G. West, op. cit., p. 114.

[11] *Saturday Review*, 29 January 1898, p. 147.

[12] Reprinted in *Certain Personal Matters*, 1898 [1897], pp. 172–9. See also 'Another Early Wells Item' by the present writer, *Nineteenth Century Fiction*, xiii (1958), 72–3.

[13] *Certain Personal Matters*, pp. 178–9.

[14] Representative examples from the seventies and eighties include *The Battle of Dorking* by Sir George Chesney (1871), first published anonymously, as were most publications of this kind; *The Battle of Pluck* (1875); *The Invasion of 1883* (1876); *How John Bull Lost London* by 'Grip' (1882); *The Invasion of England* by Sir William Butler (1882); *The Siege of London* by 'Posteritas' (1885); *The Great Naval War of 1887* (n.d., c. 1886); and *The Battle Off Worthing* (1887). During the nineties and early nineteen-hundreds there appeared such works as *The Great War of 189–: A Forecast* by P. Colomb and others (1893); *The Great War in England in 1897* by William Le Quex (1894); *The Great Anglo-American War of 1900* (1896); *The Final War* by Louis Tracy (1896) and the same author's *The Invaders* (1900); *The Yellow Danger* by M. P. Shiel (1898); *The New Battle of Dorking* by F. N. Maude (1900); and *How the Germans Took London* by T. W. Offin (1900).

[15] Elie Halévy, *A History of the English People in the Nineteenth Century*, V, 1951, viii.

[16] 'The Novels of Mr George Gissing', *Contemporary Review*, lxxii (1897), 200.

CHAPTER VI

[1] 'The Romance of the Scientist', *The Young Man*, op. cit., p. 256.

[2] *Royal College of Science Magazine*, April 1903, p. 223.

[3] *The Sleeper Awakes*, 1910, p. ii.

[4] *Speaker*, 3 June 1899, p. 639.

[5] *Athenaeum*, 3 June 1899, p. 685.

[6] *Academy*, 10 June 1899, p. 624.

[7] *A Modern Utopia*, 1905, p. v.

[8] *New York Herald*, 15 April 1906.

[9] *Academy*, 10 June 1899.

[10] *Academy*, op. cit.

[11] *The Future in America*, 1906, pp. 11–12.

[12] *Anticipations*, 1901, pp. 39–40.

[13] A. L. Morton, *The English Utopia*, 1952, p. 192.

[14] *The Sleeper Awakes*, 1910, p. ii.

[15] *Anticipations*, 1901, pp. 147–8.

[16] Ibid., pp. 79–80.

[17] *The Sleeper Awakes*, 1910, p. i.

[18] *Experiment in Autobiography*, II, 459–60, 587.

[19] *Athenaeum*, 14 December, 1901, p. 807.

[20] *Works* (Atlantic Edition, 1924), VI, ix.

[21] 'Jules Verne Revisited', *T.P.'s Weekly*, 9 October 1903, p. 589.

[22] Norman Nicholson, *H. G. Wells*, 1950, p. 25.

[23] 'Views and Reviews', *New English Weekly*, 8 February 1940, p. 237.

[24] Nicholson, op. cit., p. 28.

[25] *The Anatomy of Frustration*, 1936, p. 7.

[26] *Academy*, 7 December 1901, p. 541.

CHAPTER VII

[1] *The Great Tradition*, 1948, p. 7.

[2] In 'The Contemporary Novel', *An Englishman Looks at the World*, 1914, p. 163.

[3] G. K. Chesterton, *Criticisms and Appreciations of Charles Dickens*, 1911, p. 52.

[4] *Arnold Bennett and H. G. Wells* (ed. Harris Wilson), 1960, pp. 45–6.

[5] *Experiment in Autobiography*, II, 601.

[6] *Autobiography*, 1936, p. 223.

[7] *The Puritan*, i (1899), 220.

[8] *Principles and Persuasions*, p. 14.

[9] Ibid., p. 14.

[10] Huxley, op. cit., p. 124.

[11] *Heretics*, 1905, p. 79.

INDEX

221

INDEX